EVANGELIZATION
and
JUSTICE

EVANGELIZATION

and

JUSTICE

NEW INSIGHTS FOR
CHRISTIAN MINISTRY

John Walsh, M.M.

ORBIS BOOKS

Maryknoll, New York 10545

Fifth Printing, December 1992

The Catholic Foreign Mission Society of America (Maryknoll) recruits and trains people for overseas missionary service. Through Orbis Books Maryknoll aims to foster the international dialogue that is essential to mission. The books published, however, reflect the opinions of their authors and are not meant to represent the official position of the society.

Copyright © 1982 by Orbis Books, Maryknoll, NY 10545
All rights reserved
Manufactured in the United States of America

Manuscript Editor: Robert Cunningham

Portions of this book originally appeared in *Ministries* (now called *Modern Ministries*), February and March 1980

Library of Congress Cataloging in Publication Data

Walsh, John J., 1933-
  Evangelization and justice.

  Bibliography: p.
  1. Pastoral theology—Catholic Church.
2. Christianity—20th century. 3. Evangelistic
work. 4. Justice. 5. Peace. I. Title.
BX1913.W28   253   82-6279
ISBN 0-88344-109-8 (pbk.)   AACR2

CONTENTS

FOREWORD, by James J. DiGiacomo, S.J.   ix

PREFACE   xi

Chapter 1
CULTURAL CHRISTIANITY: A DIAGNOSIS   1
The Problems of Cultural Christians   1
Fowler's Stages of Faith Maturity   3
The Seven Categories of Fowler's Stages   7
Shift in Megacultural Christianity   11

Chapter 2
ADDITIONAL DIAGNOSTIC IMPLICATIONS:
EVOLVE OR PERISH!   16

Chapter 3
HELPING PEOPLE EVOLVE:
ENCOUNTER INTUITION   22
The Logic of Love versus Computer Logic   22
Lonergan's Four Operations of the Human Psyche   24
Value Statements   27

Chapter 4
HELPING PEOPLE EVOLVE:
SURFACING AND EXPANDING
THE BASIC WISHES OF THE HUMAN HEART   28
A Fatal Assumption about Religion   28
What Is Religion?   29
Our Four Basic Wishes   30

Chapter 5
HELPING PEOPLE EVOLVE:
THE EVOLUTIONARY MIND-SET   33
  The Key to the Future   33
  Plato's View of Time   34
  Thomas Aquinas's Quantum Leap   34
  Teilhard de Chardin's Views   35
  The Challenge of Present-day Ministry   36

Chapter 6
THE ULTIMATE EVOLUTION:
FORETASTE NOW   39
  The Fullness of Evolution   40
  Our Ultimate Goal   40
  The Trinity as a Prophecy   42
  Christ the Evolver   44

Chapter 7
IMPLICATIONS FOR JUSTICE AND PEACE   46
  The Need to Uncover the Sources of Problems   46
  Power and the Violation of Human Rights   48
  Our Encounter with Christ the Evolver   49
  Within the Church   50
  The Imperial Model of the Church   50
  The Need for a New Model   51

Chapter 8
IMPLICATIONS FOR THE FUTURE
CHRISTIAN COMMUNITY   53
  The Characteristics of Different Groups   53
  A New Process of Evangelization   56

Chapter 9
THE SUCCESSFUL EVANGELIZER   62
  Methods of Ministry Used Prior to the Mid-sixties   64
  Methods of Ministry Used Since the Mid-sixties   64
  New Evangelization Methods   65

NOTES   69

Appendix A
JUSTICE AND PEACE:
THE CONSCIENTIZATION OF THE CHURCH   71

Appendix B
ADDITIONAL READINGS AND RESOURCES   105

FOREWORD

During great cultural shifts, when the conventional supports of religion slip away, those who would engage in Christian ministry face unaccustomed challenges. For the last two decades in the life of the American church, the attainment of religious identity has become uncommonly difficult for many who in earlier times might have easily settled into the places assigned them in the Christian community. At such times ministers of the Word often feel like foreign missionaries in their own land, speaking to people who can either no longer hear or who have ceased to listen.

So it is not surprising that help should come from a missionary. John Walsh's experience in Japan forced him to ask the really basic questions that often elude those who serve established churches. How do people come to faith? What starts them on the religious quest? In the absence or decline of conventional religiosity, how can they become Christians by personal conviction and decision? Such questions, which go to the very roots of religious experience and concern, are no longer the special preserve of the foreign missionary: the missions have come home.

This book sees the minister as a kind of physician who needs new healing skills to administer to a new kind of sickness. The patient is identified as the cultural Christian who suffers from spiritual malnutrition. Although this undernourishment is sometimes brought on by ingesting religious junk food, the more likely cause is a loss of appetite for serious religious nourishment and an inability to keep even good food down. The prescription? Discreet doses of evangelization.

"Evangelization" sounds like the latest Catholic buzz word. But it is really a very old word with a long and venerable history in the Christian community. It means "announcing the good news", and who can be against that? But to some it conjures up visions of high-pressure, pulpit-pounding preachers, and bombastic, Bible-brandishing browbeaters. What it really means is, "getting back to basics"—not repeating dogmatic formulas in catechism style, nor attempting an undesirable and impossible nostalgia trip to the lost world of the Baltimore Catechism, but getting back to basics in a more radical and authentic sense.

There are many reasons why people are bored by religion. Sometimes it is just that what goes on in church is poorly done, lacking enthusiasm or imagination. But often the reason goes much deeper. Some people cannot bear to hear the gospel, and are turned off by the church because they have not asked the questions that Jesus came to answer and have not desired the things that Jesus came to give. Until we ask those questions and seek those things, God is irrelevant, Jesus is a harmless humanist, and the church is a bore.

People no longer go to church just because "it's expected of them." Religion must be perceived as an enrichment. God must be seen, not as a master whose arbitrary demands must be grudgingly obeyed, but as the only One who can satisfy our deepest longings. St. Augustine said that our hearts are restless until they rest in him, but that statement is by no means clear to everyone.

A young religious enthusiast once wrote on his college classroom chalkboard: "Jesus Christ is the answer!" On returning later, he found that someone had written: "But what's the question?" Evangelization, when it is done well, avoids the mistake of trying to give people answers to religious questions they have not asked. It addresses those who question not only the truth of Christianity but also the relevance of the religious question itself. This is indeed getting down to basics—to real depth. On such a foundation something more solid than cultural Christianity can be built. And the church will be well served if ministers can find in these pages the ability to help people hear the saving word they bring.

Crises are times not only of danger but of opportunity. John Walsh's work is a hopeful book. It can help those in ministry to recognize the danger and to seize the opportunity. It could contribute to the end of a decline and the beginning of a new vitality in sharing the Word of God.

James J. DiGiacomo, S.J.

PREFACE

When the British army surrendered at Yorktown, effectively ending the Revolutionary War, the band played a tune entitled "The World Turned Upside Down." One era had ended, another had begun.

This tune could well be the theme song of those in ministry today. They are trained to work with people who believe and practice, and now they face many who are not sure what they believe or who may have ceased the practice of their faith. Even those who believe and practice are in confusion and turmoil. In short, this is a time of crisis. One era is ending, another is beginning.

This book opens with a diagnosis of what has been happening to cultural Christianity since the mid-sixties. We also offer an overview of the possibilities for ministry in the next twenty years. During this time we shall complete not only another century of Christianity but also the second Christian millennium, and lay the groundwork for the third millennium.

In light of the preceding analysis, we shall examine certain dynamics of evangelization and their impact for ministry. This is followed by an investigation of the implications of evangelization for justice and peace, for future community, and for the self-image of persons engaged in ministry.

This handbook is not intended to be just one more how-to-do-it book, but rather a presentation of new ministerial insights gained by working closely with people engaged in ministry on four continents. I hope that a close study of this book could influence the way our ministry is carried out for years to come. It has application for all forms of educational and pastoral ministry.

The Maryknoll Constitution gives the following definition of the purpose of the society:

As an essential and integral element of its missionary activity, the Society shall stimulate and facilitate the communication and exchange of values, experiences and services between the local Churches and the Church of the United States for their mutual enrichment.[1]

Here we can note an enlarged definition of the role of the missioner. The missioner is seen as a bridge between countries, and traffic across the bridge flows in both directions.

Why should Maryknoll respond to the crisis of the church of the United States? There is, of course, a pragmatic reason. A great source of all Maryknoll's personnel and support is the sending church of the United States. If the church of the United States falters, Maryknoll will feel the effects. The motivation for Maryknoll's response to the crisis, however, lies deeper. The missioner serves as a bridge for mutual enrichment between sending and receiving churches. Just as the church of the United States is a sending church via Maryknoll, so it must also be a receiving church via Maryknoll, especially in this time of crisis.

Mutual enrichment is evident in all healthy human relationships. The basic love relationships of this world—parent and child, lover and beloved, friend and friend—often start as one-way affairs. They only reach depth, fullness, and maturity when they become reciprocal. All of these, in turn, mirror the mutual giving and receiving of the inner love-life of God in the Trinity.

We feel that three results will gradually emerge from this mission education (mission feedback, if you will). First, the gradual spreading of the evangelization process throughout the United States will be an important aid to Maryknoll's sending church in a time of crisis.

Second, the Christians of the United States will come to realize that the missioner is not engaged in some strange and exotic work that has little to do with their own lives in the United States—something like the astronauts on the moon. Instead, they will understand that we are all engaged in the same vital process: evangelization. This understanding should result in a greater awareness and appreciation of mission work.

Third, there will be an awakening or an increase of interest in work for justice and peace. For it is a sad fact that many Christians of the United States have little or no interest in activity on behalf of justice and peace. Once we have gone through the evangelization process, we shall see devotion to justice and peace as one of the central roles of the Christian life. We look forward then to a greater involvement of U.S. Christians in this vital action.

In order to obtain the full impact of this small book, you have to not only read it but also to reflect and meditate on its message.

May the Holy Spirit bring a new sense of adventure and romance into our Christian ministry!

EVANGELIZATION
and
JUSTICE

Chapter 1

CULTURAL CHRISTIANITY: A DIAGNOSIS

Nearly everyone agrees that cultural Christianity is today in a period of transition. But cultural Christians—those who are born as Christians into a Christian environment—do not seem to agree as to whether this development is good or bad. Some feel that we are going to hell in a handbasket. Others believe that great things are happening. Few would claim that we are still doing "business as usual."

The Problems of Cultural Christians

Who are these cultural Christians caught up in a cultural Christianity that is in flux? The answer is: We are, and so are most of the people to whom we minister. Imagine, if you will, a person who enters Christianity as an adult. Sometime after becoming a Christian he or she marries another Christian. They then proceed to raise a family with which they share the Christian heritage. The Christian convert and the children arrive at Christianity in radically different ways. The convert does so after a series of search-and-encounter experiences. The children (and grandchildren) arrive at Christianity by being born into a Christian environment —their immediate family and the Christians who surround it. As

1

these born Christians grow up, they are gradually introduced to Christian practices and beliefs. The convert, on the other hand, arrives at Christianity through a searching that emanates from "inside." The children arrive at Christianity from a sharing of a heritage that comes from "outside."

As long as the environment—cultural Christianity—of born Christians, i.e., cultural Christians, remains stable, things work rather well. Born Christians rejoice in a security and certainty that nurtures Christian life in both childhood and adulthood. If, however, cultural Christianity itself begins to shift, many kinds of problems arise.

In 1976 Father Philip Murnion, a priest-sociologist in the Archdiocese of New York, conducted a survey of the religious attitudes of Catholics in the Yorkville section of Manhattan. He found that 41 percent of the area's Catholics who do not attend Mass do not believe in a personal God.[2] Not only have they ceased all church practice but they have also ceased to believe in the church, in Christ, and in a personal God.

Even cultural Christians who continue to practice their faith find themselves in turmoil when the environment changes. Some may ask, "Why can't they leave things as they were? You have to admit the church was in better shape twenty years ago!" Others may say, "Just because Christians in the past believed certain things and did certain things does that mean I have to imitate their beliefs and actions?" Almost all of us agree that cultural Christians today find themselves in a cultural Christianity in a state of transition. The question is: "Where are we going, and what exactly is happening?"

This question brings us to the distinction between symptoms and diagnosis. When you are sick, you know your symptoms better than anyone else. Your chest hurts, you have difficulty breathing, you have a fever. You know these things better than your doctor does. Yet you go to a doctor. Why? Because he or she can make sense of your symptoms. A doctor can rise above the confusion of your varied symptoms to give you an overview of what is happening. In short, a doctor can give you a diagnosis.

Can we do the same thing for cultural Christianity? Can we rise above the smoke of battle to diagnose what has been happening in cultural Christianity since the mid-sixties? Is it possible in this way to throw some light on what might happen in the last twenty years of the twentieth century? I believe we can. We do, however, need a diagnostic tool. To this end let us examine James Fowler's theory of the Stages of Faith Maturity.[3]

Fowler's Stages of Faith Maturity

It is a grave injustice to try to sum up in a few paragraphs the results of long years of work by an eminent thinker like Fowler. What follows, therefore, is only a very general presentation of his theory. In 1968–69 Fowler was associate director of Interpreter's House, a center in North Carolina for the continuing education of members of the clergy and for retreats for lay persons. During his year at Interpreter's House, Fowler listened to over two hundred life stories containing accounts of people's faith experiences. As he listened, he began to uncover, amid a great variety of individual details, certain patterns of faith transformation. This initial insight became the nucleus of his theory of religious development. In the fall of 1969, Fowler began to teach at Harvard Divinity School. Here he began his formal research into the theory of the Stages of Faith Maturity. Building on the work of the well-known psychologists Jean Piaget, Erik Erikson, and Lawrence Kohlberg, Fowler began to delineate more sharply the characteristics of various stages of faith development.[4] At present he is continuing his research at Emory University in Atlanta.

Fowler does not see faith as a noun but rather as a verb. He defines faith as active "mode-of-being-in-relation" to the Other or others, accompanied by belief, commitment, love, and risk. Faith encompasses our most essential images and actions in relation to the ultimate reality, coherence, and purpose of life. Faith is a person's or a community's mode-of-being-in-relation to what we might call our ultimate environment.

Let us now begin to examine Fowler's Stages of Faith Maturity with respect to the lives of cultural Christians. It goes without saying that the faith of cultural Christians comes from God, but God works in an incarnational way:

THE STAGES OF FAITH MATURITY

Stage One:	Intuitive-projective	Faith from parents (moods and actions)
Stage Two:	Mythic-literal	Faith from parents/parent substitute ("stories")
Stage Three:	Synthetic-conventional	Faith from environment (group)
Stage Four:	Individuating-reflexive	Individuals begin to be responsible for their own faith (polarities arise)
Stage Five:	Conjunctive or Paradoxical-consolidative	Individuals absorb good from opposite polarities
Stage Six:	Universalizing	Resolution/Superanimation of all polarities

The first stage extends from infancy to approximately age six. In this stage we receive our faith from our parents, not by formal teaching but by picking up the basic parental attitudes toward God, Christ, prayer, the church, and so on. This learning is by "osmosis," as it were, much as we learn to speak.

The second stage generally extends from age seven to twelve. In this stage we receive our faith from a parent or parent substitute—a brother, sister, priest, or lay religion teacher. These people pass on to us the "stories" of Christianity. "Stories" is used here in a very wide sense that is not limited to Bible stories. Rather it means that this is what we Christians believe; this is what we Christians do. We are now passing these beliefs and these actions on to you in simple literal form. You are the oncoming generation, and so we share our Christian heritage with you.

The third stage begins at about age thirteen, and for many it extends right through adulthood. In this stage we receive our faith from our environment or group. We feel that we have been born into a winning group—in this case, Christians. To be more specific, we have been born as Episcopalians, Lutherans, or Catholics.

The game plan in life at this stage is to get into the *middle* of a group and stay there. In this stage people do not want to be either too far out in front or too far in the rear. They want to be loyal members, that is, team players. They want to learn what the group teaches and do what the group does. They do not have to know all the answers. There is security in the group—the herd instinct, if you will.

It would seem that until the mid-sixties, most cultural Christians moved through Fowler's first two stages, attained the third stage in their teens, and then lived and died in that stage. We need to keep in mind that they had successful Christian lives. This last point is most important, as will be explained later.

Some people never move on to Fowler's fourth stage, although the shift from Stage Three to Stage Four can begin as early as age sixteen. This does not mean that people can immediately enter Stage Four. Rather it means that they now have sufficient life experiences and potentiality to start to leave Stage Three and to begin the journey toward Stage Four, a journey that may take many years. Although sixteen can be considered the minimal age, adults may start to leave Stage Three at any age. Unfortunately, many of us never move beyond Stage Three.

For those of us who move on to Stage Four, the transition goes something like this: At a given moment we realize that eventually we will have to look Christ Jesus in the eye and account for our lives. At that time we will not be able to hide in our group and say, "Well, the group didn't think this was important. The group neglected such-and-such." No, we will have to account to Christ for our own actions and systems of values.

In light of this awareness, we may begin to assume responsibility for our own faith system. This does not mean that we will reject out-of-hand the faith system we had in the third stage. It means that we now have to go through an agonizing reappraisal in order to authenticate and personalize what we had in the third stage.

This does not mean that we will go off to a mountaintop in

splendid isolation and come down a few years later with our own private interpretation of the meaning of life. It means that we must pray intensely to the Spirit that the gospel may come alive for us. It means that we have to realize our need for others and for their support and counsel. Paradoxically, leaving Stage Three (the stage of the group) does not mean that we will become less community-minded. It means that we shall feel an even greater need for community—a community of fellow seekers.

As we go through this agony of reappraisal, a series of polarities will form. Every criterion in assuming responsibility for our own faith has its countercriterion. Every instrument by which we measure has its counterinstrument. Let's consider some examples:

1. Do we work through this change just by means of logic, or do we rely on our deepest feelings and intuitions?

2. Do we consider the organization the most important thing, even if some people get ground up in the gears? Or are individuals all-important?

3. Are our own spiritual lives of prime importance, or is our service to others the thing that counts?

The list is endless. In Fowler's fourth stage, people generally cannot cope with both sets of criteria. They tend to cling to one set and throw away the other. In a meeting or discussion group, of course, they still pay lip service to the other set. But if you wake them up at three o'clock in the morning and shine a flashlight in their eyes, they will probably tell you truthfully which set of criteria is important to them. They may also admit that they don't care for the other set at all!

The fifth stage can be attained at about age thirty. Thirty is the minimal age, but many who attain this stage do so only at a later age. In the fifth stage we can absorb good from the opposite set of polarities. At first glance it might appear that we have become theological Charlie Browns, oozing a wishy-washy acceptance in all directions: "Oh, this is fine; oh, that's fine also; everything is fine!" We may seem to have become fence straddlers—a kind of theological jello flowing in every direction. But this is not the case at all. Once we have attained Stage Five, we have become mature, liberated persons, for now we can deal with paradox and dialectic: logic *and* intuition, organization *and* individual uniqueness, loyalty *and* independence, and so on. We can draw good from polarities: This is akin to the use of muscles in the arm. We have muscles on one side of our arms that pull in one direction and muscles on the other side that pull in the opposite direction. Because of these opposing sets of muscles, our arm can move in every direction. In the fifth stage we also can move freely—at times, of course, with difficulty—but a whole new world is now open to us.

The minimal age for attaining the sixth stage is about thirty-eight. Fowler says very few of us ever attain Stage Six. Most of us get bogged down somewhere along the line. If we do attain Stage Six, we now experience a resolution of all polarities. But this stage involves much more than just a resolution of polarities. The person in Stage Six is very much a God-lover, very much a people-lover, very much a community person, very much a strong individual, a pioneer, wonder-full, a barrier-breaker—in short, a Saint Paul type. A rare person indeed!

The Seven Categories of Fowler's Stages

Each one of Fowler's six stages contains seven categories by which the stages are explained:

> Form of Logic
> Form of World Coherence
> Role Taking
> Locus of Authority
> Bounds of Social Awareness
> Form of Moral Judgment
> Role of Symbols

Let us briefly examine each of these categories. Following a description of each category there will be examples from Stages Three, Four, and Five, which are the pivotal stages of Fowler's theory. As will be seen, these categories are not watertight compartments; there is a certain amount of overlapping. The categories should be seen as points of focus within each stage.

Form of Logic. This category is a modified form of Piaget's theory of cognitive development.[5] It is based on the patterns of reasoning and judgment used by us as individuals.

In Stage Three we begin to reflect on our own thinking and valuing. There is great emphasis on making sure that our personal thinking and valuing are in accordance with that of the most important people in our group.

In Stage Four the reflection on personal thinking and valuing emphasizes the need to reflect reality even if that means challenging some of the customs of our group. At this stage, however, we cannot cope with all the criteria available for making value judgments. Some criteria are accepted; others are rejected. As a result, we tend to think in a dichotomizing way. There is an either/or mentality with a clinging to polarities.

In Stage Five our thinking and judgment take on an integrating factor. A creative tension leading to ever greater insights can be maintained between polarities. Our cognitive operations are now able to function with a dialectical style of thinking and valuing.

Form of World Coherence. This category deals with our attempts to form cohesive patterns in viewing the meaning of life.

In Stage Three we accept the worldview of the group into which we were born. This view is accepted in a noncritical way with little or no evaluation. Without much questioning, the social, economic, and political systems in which we are situated are accepted. They are because they are.

In Stage Four, however, authenticity and consistency become important. Our perspective is broadened even if that means meeting with challenge and change. There is an ability to assume responsibility for our own views.

In Stage Five our worldview becomes more pluralistic. We recognize that no single view has *all* the truth. Reductionist viewpoints are set aside. Fowler feels that people who have suffered discrimination are able to attain this pluralistic viewpoint more quickly than those who have always had a position of advantage.

Role Taking. This category is a modified form of the research done by Robert Selman of the Harvard Graduate School of Education.[6] It investigates our ability to take on the perspective, first of our own group, and then that of groups beyond our own.

In Stage Three our perspective is limited to our own group. We consider who are the significant people in this group and try to the best of our ability to correspond to their perspectives.

In Stage Four our perspective goes beyond the limits of the original group. Our outlook is indeed broadened, but we still tend to cling to polarities.

In Stage Five, however, we are better able to transcend our personal views in order to encompass the perspectives of persons in many other groups and to enter into fruitful dialogue with them.

Locus of Authority. Here we are dealing with how we accept the viewpoint of authority.

In Stage Three we tend to be conformists, following without question what authorities say. Authorities must be right because they are *the* persons in authority.

In Stage Four we feel the necessity to assume responsibility for our own evaluating and commitment: "I can no longer follow blindly. I must monitor my own judgments and take responsibility for my own actions."

In Stage Five the viewpoint of authority is given serious consideration, but it must be subjected to evaluation by being placed into a dialectical relationship with higher principles of action.

Bounds of Social Awareness. As the term suggests, this category deals with the extent of our social responsibility.

In Stage Three we are addicted to tribalism. Our interest extends only to our group. We will make many sacrifices for the immediate group, but the problems of those outside the group are of little consequence.

In Stage Four our social awareness will extend beyond our own group. We are now willing to reach out to those in other racial, class, or national groups. This outreach will extend to groups with which we now feel an affinity, but it will not extend to all groups.

In Stage Five, however, we are better able to transcend barriers; hence, we have an even greater social outreach to many groups.

Form of Moral Judgment. This is a modified form of Kohlberg's theory of moral development.[7]

In Stage Three we are still in Kohlberg's conventional stages (Kohlberg Stage 3 or Stage 4). There is a desire to maintain rules that enforce a stereotyped good behavior. There is a fear that change will break down the system with its defined rules and roles.

In Stage Four the situation approximates Kohlberg's Stage 5, which is postconventional. We are striving for the principles of an ideal of justice, but still carry a certain amount of group bias.

In Stage Five we are trying to fulfill a consistent higher-law perspective in both judgment (what is to be done) and action (carrying it out).

Role of Symbols. This category deals with our ability to use symbols, myths, and rituals in helping to interpret the meaning of life.

In Stage Three the use of symbols is precritical. The accepted symbols and rituals of the group are used without much evaluation. This is a conventional use of symbols.

In Stage Four there is a critical demythologizing of symbols. In this stage symbols are used as a matrix to provide ideas and concepts regarding the purpose of life.

In Stage Five, however, symbols are again used as a source for intellectual construction. But along with this use is associated an affective element. Symbols are also seen as providing insight, intuition, and experience that cannot be captured by intellect alone. Hence, there is a return (albeit now on a much more sophisticated level) to the way in which symbols, myths, and rituals were used at the primal level of Fowler's Stages One and Two.

From discussions with Fowler and from listening to many people in my own work, it seems to me that some people are "between" stages. Some will say, "I feel schizophrenic. Some days I think I am in Fowler's Stage Three; some days I feel I am in Stage Four." Others will say, "At times I operate as a person in the fourth stage, and at other times I find myself operating in the fifth stage." It goes without saying that a full transition from one stage to another can only take place over an extended period of time. It seems that when we advance from one stage to the next, we make great progress in some of the above categories, while in others we may lag behind. Hence, while operating in certain categories, we feel that we are in the higher stage. And when operating in other categories, we feel stranded in the lower stage.

Shift in Megacultural Christianity

Let us remember that we began this consideration of Fowler's stages as a diagnostic tool to discover what has been happening in cultural Christianity since the mid-sixties, and to predict in some small way what will happen in the next twenty years. I believe that not only individuals go through Fowler's stages but that whole cultures as well go through the stages—in this case, cultural Christianity. What seems to be happening now is that cultural Christianity as a whole is moving from Fowler's Stage Three into Stage Four. The transition began in the mid-sixties, and will possibly go on until the turn of the century.

Throughout the history of Christianity we have always had individuals dispersed among all of Fowler's stages. What is happening now is that cultural Christianity *as a whole* is moving from the third stage into the fourth.

The description given above of Fowler's Stage Three seems to be a good working description of cultural Christianity prior to the mid-sixties. At that time society was saying to us:

Look, you were born a Catholic (or Protestant or Jew); be a good one. If you're a Catholic, you should go to Mass on Sunday. You should study what you are taught, do what you are commanded, and believe as you are instructed. And if you are really keen on these things, you should go off to become a brother, sister, or priest.

Is not the above description of Fowler's Stage Four a good working description of what is happening now? What is society now saying to us? It is saying, "You rise or fall on your own basic convictions; you have to assume responsibility for your own faith system." It is Fowler's Stage Four message. Faced with this imperative, some of us are confused, others are slowly bleeding to death, and many have ceased to practice their religion.

This shift from Stage Three to Stage Four is taking place in what we might call megacultural Christianity: Europe, North and South America, the Philippines, Australia, New Zealand, and the pockets of born Christians in Asia and Africa. Each individual country or community may have its own particular schedule for transition—some a little faster, some a little slower—but they are all moving. It is like a river that flows over a waterfall. Given a series of boats on a river, some will reach the waterfall before others, but in the end all of them must come to the falls. Some people may buy time by jumping upstream from boat to boat, but eventually all must go over the waterfall.

Actually, the shift from Stage Three to Stage Four began in parts of Europe prior to the mid-sixties. In the early sixties we in the United States were praying like the Pharisee in the Temple, "O God, we thank you that we are not like the French or the Dutch. We have no big theological problems; our people are going to church." But in a few years it all began to happen to us. And so it goes—first in parts of Europe, then in the United States, and now more and more throughout all of cultural Christianity. (Actually, some of the earliest manifestations of this shift appeared in Third World countries. The *articulation* of it was clearer in Europe during the fifties and early sixties.)

Moreover, this shift from Stage Three to Stage Four goes beyond Christianity. People of all faiths at this time are faced with the imperative to rise or fall on their own basic convictions, for this process appears to be spreading gradually throughout the psychic envelope of the globe.

What brought about this change? We might bring in a team of sociologists who would give us many secondary reasons—our ability to have an almost instant communication of ideas and events throughout the world, the Vietnam crisis, Vatican II, and so on. But the primary reason, expressed in Christian terms, would be that the cosmic Christ is gradually evolving the world, bringing the world to maturity, preparing us and the world for the fullness of time and for his Second Coming. This does not mean that the Parousia is just around the corner, but that Christ is drawing us on.

The world, unfortunately, does not evolve at a steady, even pace. If it did, all of this would be much easier to understand. Instead, the world evolves in spurts, in quantum leaps, much as we do in growing up.

Perhaps the last quantum leap in Christianity took place when we came out of the Middle Ages into the Renaissance. In the Middle Ages the world known to Europeans was not only Christian but also Catholic. There were some Muslims on the fringe of Christendom, but theologians by definition cast all heretics and infidels into hell. So the Muslims didn't count. Everything in the Middle Ages was more or less in its place, and Christianity worked well—or rather people at that time thought that it was working well. Then Christians began to discover new worlds, not only North and South America, but also India and China— countries whose cultures were far superior to Europe's at the time, even though they were "pagan" lands. Christians also began to rediscover the ancient Greek and Roman culture, which was superior to the culture of the European Middle Ages, even though the culture of Antiquity was "pagan." Scientific discoveries appeared to challenge the teachings of the Bible. Many people in the church felt threatened by all these changes and wanted to preserve the old system. They said, "It worked for hundreds of years. Let's keep Christianity as it is." Others felt that the Christian world had to move on. And move on it did—not as well as it should have but Christians produced many theological and spiritual breakthroughs and initiated a golden age of missionary activity that brought Christ to new peoples all over the globe.

Once again we are in one of those times of a quantum leap. Many Christians are again crying out, "Let us keep the old system. It worked for hundreds of years." Some, however, are saying, "No, we must move on. Christianity must evolve." It goes without saying that it would be easier—at least for a time—to hold fast. The situation is somewhat akin to dealing with twelve-year-olds. We can talk to them, and they are respectful. They are nice people. But then comes the quantum leap of early adolescence, and we are left feeling that perhaps thirteen-, fourteen-, and fifteen-year-olds have reverted to the animal stage! Yet there is progress, true progress. Of course, it is painful. But we realize that unless youngsters go through this difficult time, they will never attain adulthood.

So it is now with Christianity. We are moving out of Fowler's Stage Three into Stage Four. Again it is painful, but it is progress in the eyes of the cosmic Christ, and it should be so in our eyes.

There are many in the church today who want to cling to Stage

Three. They may claim to favor change, but in the light of what was said above, the changes they would consent to would in reality be only cosmetic changes. They want to put makeup on a twelve-year-old and call that child an adult. It takes more than cosmetics to change a twelve-year-old into an adult.

This evolution to a Stage Four church is no easy transition. Let us recall that adolescence comes before adulthood. One of the characteristics of Stage Four makes this obvious. As pointed out, Stage Four is a time of clinging to one set of criteria while feeling negative toward the opposite criteria. This is why there are so many arguments going on in the church today. There are those who want to cling to Stage Three, which would seem to be an untenable position. Then there are those who are clinging to opposite sets of criteria found in Stage Four. The argument between the two camps in Stage Four is painful and at times strident, but at least the process is healthy and maturing.

Though the young always talk about being free—citizens of "the land of the free and the home of the brave," many young people today are terrified by the ongoing shift to Stage Four. They are looking desperately for Stage Three wombs in which to hide. Hence the popularity of cults. Some proclaim, "Join the Moonies, turn off the switch on your brain, and you will be told what to do and when to do it." And we have had a womb for adults that started as a caricature and ended up as a terrible tragedy: Jonestown.

Some of our seminaries and convents still offer Stage Three sanctuaries; it is no surprise that they are still getting a number of vocations. Given the shortage of vocations, other communities are tempted to construct Stage Three refuges in a world struggling toward Stage Four, but they wisely resist the temptation. They realize that with every tick of the clock such a refuge becomes less tenable. With every tick of the clock the walls of the mental ghetto mount higher until in the end the leaders of such a refuge would be running a dinosaur farm.

As has been said, until the mid-sixties most Christians lived and died in Stage Three. In all truth they had successful Christian lives. As long as our culture remained in Stage Three, all we had to do to have viable lives as Christians was to attain that stage. Now, however, all of us must match our evolving culture and strive for

Stage Four. We all have a vocation to Stage Four so that we may live fuller lives as Christians. And, of course, those of us who are in ministry are not above all this. It is also our vocation. In fact, those in ministry should strive for Stage Five because only a person who is able to absorb good from opposite sets of polarities will be able to minister well to people in Stage Four who tend to cling to just one set of polarities. (This is not to suggest an elitism: those in ministry in Stage Five are above the "ordinary" folk in Stage Four. If one is Christian, one is called to ministry—of some sort. The more people who attain Stage Five (or Six) the better.) We must understand that in virtue of our ministry we are being called by Christ to do this. As ministers to others, we must first minister to ourselves.

Chapter 2

ADDITIONAL DIAGNOSTIC IMPLICATIONS: EVOLVE OR PERISH!

In light of the first chapter, we can now assemble a series of further diagnostic insights that are at our disposal:

1. We have the beginnings of a shared vocabulary. It becomes much easier to discuss problems of ministry once an overview and its attendant vocabulary are attained.

2. Perhaps for the first time we can get to the heart of the matter and not merely deal with the symptoms of problems. As stated previously, when we are sick, we know our symptoms better than anyone else, yet we go to the doctor. Why? Because if we don't, we merely treat the symptoms. We drink liquids for our fever, we take aspirin for the pain in our chest, we lie down so that it becomes easier to breathe. But we are not getting any better! So off we go to the doctor, who may discover that we have pneumonia. That's not exactly pleasant news, but at least we now know what the real problem is and we can begin to do something about it.

In an analogous way this is what has happened to us in ministry in recent years. We have become so concerned with the symptoms —people no longer going to Mass and so forth—that we have not really been able to understand what basically was happening—a quantum leap in the culture based on how we arrive at a system of faith/life values. We conformed to George Santayana's definition of fanaticism, and redoubled our efforts while forgetting our aims.

3. As we have seen, the shift from Stage Three to Stage Four can begin as early as age sixteen, when we have the potentiality to start to leave Stage Three and begin the journey to Stage Four. This journey may take several years and is not a problem just for older adolescents. Most Christian adults have bogged down either in Stage Three or somewhere between Stages Three and Four. Hence, the challenge is not just for the young but also for the young-at-heart of all ages.

4. For those ministering to younger adolescents in Stage Three, the situation has serious implications. Generally we enter the third stage at about age thirteen. It goes without saying that we cannot progress to Stage Four until we have first gone through Stage Three. Prior to the mid-sixties, the third stage was the final stage most people attained, and so we brought young adolescents into this stage by *formation through information*. We said:

> Here are the truths of your religion (that is, the Baltimore Catechism). They are carved in stone; they will do you for the rest of your life. Put them in your knapsack and they will see you through to heaven.

And it worked. As long as cultural Christianity itself was in Stage Three, it worked. Now that each of us has a vocation to Stage Four, Stage Three becomes a transitional stage, not a final stage. Stage Three now becomes *formation through transformation*. We might say:

> When you reach sixteen, you are going to begin a great Christian adventure. What we want to do for you now in early adolescence is to prepare you for that adventure by giving you the necessary religious literacy and prayer/celebrating skills. We want to prepare the rocket-launching platform so that the rocket itself may take off later in older adolescence.

5. This brings us to the question of when the sacrament of Confirmation should be administered. As long as this sacrament continues to be administered at age twelve or thirteen, what we are actually doing is confirming the youth's entrance into Stage Three. More and more, Confirmation is becoming a graduation ceremony. Many young people say:

> We've been confirmed. Why go to religion class anymore since we know all that religious information already? We don't want to hear the same material—even at a mature level—over and over again.

Once people have their driver's licenses, why should they continue to go to driving school? Confirmation should be administered at about age seventeen. By that time the young person should have begun to leave Stage Three and should have about a year's experience of the evangelization process, the vehicle by which we evolve from Stage Three to Stage Four. We would then be confirming the youth's faith into Stage Four.

6. Added to this, there is also a shift in our "virtues and vices" list. In a pure Stage Three situation prior to the mid-sixties, dependence, docility, and subjection were in vogue. At that time, while qualities such as initiative, creativity, independence, criticism (in the sense of evaluation leading to liberation) may not have been technically considered vices, they were certainly looked upon with a jaundiced eye. The Stage Three vices have now become necessary virtues for a Stage Four Christianity.

7. Paradoxically, Stage Four, in which we assume responsibility for our own faith/life values, begets a greater union in community than Stage Three (faith from the group). Let us imagine that we are situated on a satellite above the earth, and that we have been there since life began on this planet about 3.5 billion years ago. We are trying to discover God's plan for life on the earth. After a few billion years of scrutiny we feel we have uncovered the key—sameness. God makes many of his creatures alike, and the members of each species, because they are so similar, stay together and support each other. Zebras take care of zebras, crows take care of crows, and so on. We discover that all went well until a couple of million years ago when suddenly humans appeared, and

each one was different, possessing a unique personality. It seems that God deviated from his plan of sameness. Yet paradoxically God's evolving of humans led to a greater level of support and sharing because these new creatures could love.

Animal life → (survival by sameness)	Appearance of the human person (individual uniqueness)*	Paradox: a higher level of survival/being

*A dangerous but inevitable step in the evolutionary process of God's plan.

In an analogous way, the same phenomenon takes place in the transition from Stage Three to Stage Four. The basis for community in a Stage Three cultural Christianity was unity by uniformity. Stage Four seems to undermine the very foundation of community and good order. Christians are becoming different. "So much for community and church," cry some. "Sing 'Nearer My God to Thee' as the *Titanic* goes down!" Yet as we personalize and authenticate our own faith, each of us has something unique to contribute to a new type of community, one based on unity in diversity. Paradoxically again, we feel a greater need for support and counsel from the community than we did in Stage Three. But now this support comes from a community of fellow seekers. The need is now coming from the inside to the outside. Each of us thinks, "I need fellow seekers on this odyssey called life." This situation is diametrically opposed to Stage Three, where the need came from the outside to the inside. Then each of us merely thought, "By a historical accident I was born into this group."

Stage Three → (unity by uniformity)	Stage Four (individual uniqueness/ unity in diversity)*	Paradox: a higher level of union

*A dangerous but inevitable step in the evolutionary process of God's plan.

8. It is possible to remain trapped in Stage Three by a fatal flaw—our refusal to admit there are any stages beyond the third. If we use only Stage Three criteria to judge if there is anything beyond that stage, the result is a foregone conclusion: There is nothing beyond Stage Three. Doubtless, we will always admit that there is great room for progress, but it is always progress in

terms of a greater intensity of Stage Three, not progress in terms of a quantum leap into a higher stage of Christian existence.

It is like a man who owns a horse and wants to go from New York to San Francisco. Approaching the owner of an airplane, he inquires, "My horse can go one hundred miles on a bale of hay. How far can your airplane go on a bale of hay?" "Actually it can't move at all on a bale of hay," replies the airplane owner. The conclusion of the horse owner is that it is better to go to San Francisco by horse than by airplane. The mistake is that he is refusing to use anything but a "horse ruler" to measure an airplane.

It is ironic that the very qualities in which the Stage Three person glories could be counterproductive if, by a historical accident, that person happened to be born outside Christianity. Then the quality of stability and the refusal to accept the possibility of a quantum leap would keep him or her outside Christianity.

All is not darkness and gloom, however. There is a way out of this dilemma. Why do some people refuse to use anything but Stage Three criteria? There are many reasons, of course, but one prevalent reason is our fear that if we accept the possibility of Stage Four and beyond, this amounts to rejecting all that was done in the past in a Stage Three situation. If Stage Four is "right," then all that we did in Stage Three ministry and life experiences must have been "wrong."

Unfortunately, a dichotomy has been established. No one is going to accept a higher stage if the life activities of the former stage have to be renounced as a mistake. No one is going to commit psychic suicide. What must be explained to the person is that while cultural Christianity was in Stage Three, a Stage Three ministry and spirituality were, on the whole, the best for that time. But as cultural Christianity evolves, we also must evolve.

We might liken this situation to an Eskimo village where for hundreds of years people have enjoyed a happy existence by building igloos and fishing through the ice. One day an Eskimo returns to the village and announces that about twenty miles farther north he has seen water—something he had never seen before. Gradually Eskimos return from all points of the compass with the same message. It begins to dawn on the villagers that they are on an ice sheet that is moving south! If they don't soon get involved in kayaks and navigation, they are going to be in trouble. This does not mean that they have to renounce what their ancestors or they themselves have been doing as "wrong." In the past situation, what they did was the "right" thing to do. But now their world is changing, and they must evolve a new life form. As Christ draws us on in this time of quantum change, the same challenge confronts us of our attachment to the past, coupled with our need to accept what is radically new.

9. Finally, this whole development presents a great challenge to those of us in ministry. As we have seen, the last time such a quantum leap took place in cultural Christianity was when Christians came out of the Middle Ages into the Renaissance. If we are pessimists, we might say, "Just our luck! These changes take place only about every four hundred years. Just when we are ready to do our ministry, everything falls apart." If, on the other hand, we are optimists, we will say: "This is a pivotal time in Christianity and what we do in the next twenty years could have implications in Christianity for a hundred or two hundred years to come. Now that's exciting!"

Perhaps two hundred years ago the minutemen (and minute maidens!) would have rather stayed at home and worked their farms. But it was a pivotal time in politics, and, for better or worse, they created the United States. We, too, are at a pivotal time and a similar challenge faces us—this time in Christian ministry. Will we rise to the challenge? If the cosmic Christ is saying anything to us today, it is "Evolve or perish!"

Chapter 3

HELPING PEOPLE EVOLVE: ENCOUNTER INTUITION

In the preceding two chapters a diagnostic overview and its implications for cultural Christianity have been presented. Diagnosis alone, however, is not going to solve our problems in ministry. We now have to devise a prescriptive procedure. If a doctor were just to diagnose our illness and then push us out of the office, we would feel that he or she had done only half the job. We expect the doctor also to prescribe a way for us to regain our health.

In like manner what we in ministry now need is a series of dynamics that will help people evolve from Stage Three to the higher stages. It would seem that we have uncovered a series of such dynamics in our transcultural investigation of evangelization in Japan, Korea, Guatemala, Venezuela, Kenya, Tanzania, and the United States. Let us examine three dynamics of evangelization: Encounter intuition will be considered in this chapter. Surfacing and expanding the basic wishes of the human heart will be the subject of Chapter 4. The evolutionary mind-set will be discussed in Chapters 5 and 6.

The Logic of Love versus Computer Logic

How many of us have ever stopped to consider how we fall in love? Without trying to encompass this mysterious phenomenon, let us try to surface some of its characteristics. There is a leap out

22

of self toward the other person. There is a desire to encounter the other and participate in a mutual giving and receiving. There is a desire to increase the joy and being of the other, and (mystery of mysteries!) the other desires to increase our own joy and being. As the mutual giving and receiving continue in events of happiness, sorrow, and everyday activity, our reasons for entering into this greatest of all adventures become clearer. But this whole development can be fully clarified only as the result of time and experience.

What happened in the beginning that led us to initiate this adventure? That is the crux of the mystery of love. Let us examine our own love-life vis-à-vis Christ and vis-à-vis other people. First we fall in love; only later (sometimes much later) are we able to say, "How do I love thee? Let me count the ways." Why did we move toward the other long before we could count the ways? We fell in love by an outreach of our "encounter intuition." (The reader's pardon is asked for the introduction of a new term. My purpose is not to clog up further an already jargon-filled world. It was impossible to find an expression in current use that exactly encompasses what is meant by "encounter intuition.") What exactly is an encounter intuition? It is our intelligence, aided by our will and emotions, that leaps to a final conclusion—I will be open to love and encounter—without explicitly going through the intermediate steps for doing so. We do touch upon these intermediate steps in an implicit or intuitional way and, hence, our act is a human, rational one.

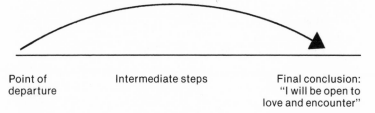

Point of   Intermediate steps   Final conclusion:
departure   "I will be open to
                                                        love and encounter"

There is a difference between the logic of love and computer logic. Imagine, if you will, a male robot falling in love. He says to himself:

There goes Suzie. Suzie looks as if she would keep a clean house, balance the budget, and prepare good meals. Suzie looks as if she would be a good mother and an asset to the neighborhood. Therefore, I will love Suzie. Suzie, will you date me?

Presumably, this is how a male robot (with a sexist silicon chip in him) might fall in love. But this is not how humans fall in love.

The robot explicitly goes through all the intermediate steps before making a move. The human heart operates differently. It is open to adventure and romance and is willing to leap out of self toward the other person. Yet how many times have we done ministry employing a computer logic? We have given people all the reasons to love Christ and others, and then we get very upset when they don't fall in love with Christ and with other human beings. This may have worked as long as we were merely socializing cultural Christians into a Stage Three cultural Christianity, but it will no longer work in a Stage Four Christianity. The logic of love and encounter intuition must now become operative.

Lonergan's Four Operations of the Human Psyche

Can we throw a little more light on just how this encounter intuition works? Bernard Longeran is one of the great authorities on how the religious psyche functions. Let us see if we can make use of some of Longeran's ideas for our pastoral purposes.[8]

Have you ever seen a model of the inside of an internal combustion engine working in slow motion in a museum? In this way, maybe for the first time, you really begin to understand what happens inside an automobile engine. In much the same way, according to Lonergan, if we examine the human psyche in slow motion, we see that it is doing one of four operations:

Experiencing
Understanding
Judging
Deciding

First we *experience* something (a movie, a pizza, a flower, another person, God, a liturgy, or a scriptural passage). We then try to *understand* the significance of it. Next we *judge* whether what we have experienced is important, boring, or interesting.

And finally we *decide* whether we want more of it, less of it, or none of it. For the most part, these operations are going on in the back of our head (or heart), and we are not paying much attention to them.

There are times, however, when we bring these operations to the front and experience them in a much more explicit and intense fashion. What is the mechanism that brings these operations from an implicit level to an explicit level? It is what we might call the "myself" principle. As long as the operations remain at the implicit level, the movie, pizza, flower, person, God, liturgy, or scriptural passage are just sitting out there and being considered in a very detached fashion. Once we begin to consider these questions—What is the significance to myself of those people/things out there? What happens if I become intimately involved with them?—we have invoked the "myself" principle. We then begin to do the four operations mentioned above in an explicit fashion. We can now add to our diagram as follows:

Implicit consciousness	*Explicit ("myself") consciousness*
	(+-)
Experiencing	Experiencing
Understanding	Understanding
Judging	Judging
Deciding	Deciding

Notice that a (+-) symbol has also been added to the diagram. What is the significance of this? Basically what all of us in ministry are doing is to say to people:

> Attention! I would like you to invoke the "myself" principle. We are going to have an experience (a liturgy, class, meeting, rap session, party, or visit). We hope you will enter into the experience, understand its significance, judge it favorably, and decide you want even more intense encounters of this type in the future.

Have you ever noticed that some people are with you right from the beginning? They have a large plus sign on their foreheads. They are attentive to the experience, try to understand its significance, are very open to a favorable judgment, and will most likely decide in favor of a future commitment.

Unfortunately, many of the people we face have a minus sign on their foreheads. They seem to go out of their way to be inattentive to the experience, are singularly obtuse as regards understanding it, are prejudiced (in the sense of prejudging it and their verdict is negative), and decide that they want no more of it. Perhaps under duress they may accept a minimum of this experience in the future because of parental or societal pressure.

We are now at the heart of the matter as regards ministry. No matter how good the experience may be, if the person has a minus sign on his or her forehead, our ministerial effort is going to fail. "But," you splutter, "I haven't even begun the liturgy (or class, or other experience). It's still only the top of the first inning!" Sorry, friend, you lose the game—unless you help the person do something about that minus sign on the forehead.

Now what is it that determines whether a plus sign or a minus sign goes on the person's forehead? Lonergan says it is a decision made at the implicit level. And so we now add the following to our diagram:

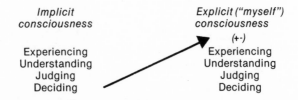

It would seem that there is a very strong correlation between the decision made at the implicit level of consciousness and the encounter intuition examined at the beginning of this chapter. Further, we have found in our transcultural investigation of evangelization that the only things that seem to motivate the encounter intuition or the implicitly conscious decisions are "value statements."

Before we investigate just what a value statement is, a warning (or explanation) is in order. We are dealing here with an encounter involving acts of love. Therefore, we must keep in mind that God's grace and human free will are present. These can never be programmed like a computer. With this caution in mind, however, it is still the duty of the sower (minister) not only to sow the seed but also to prepare the soil to receive the seed. Unfortunately, the sower often becomes so enamoured of the seed (that is, the class, liturgy, activity, or other aspect of the seed) that he or she neglects to prepare the soil. This is especially the case in this time of a quantum change in cultural Christianity. And so we come once again to the encounter intuition and value statements.

Value Statements

What is a value statement? Imagine, if you will, a non-Christian in Japan or Korea approaching you, stating that he or she knows nothing about Christianity, and then asking, "Who is Christ?" To start immediately on a discourse of complete religious information would do more harm than good. What is needed in your reply is some statement that will really get through to the inquirer—a statement that responds to a basic wish of the person's heart. A value statement is very much like one facet on the head of a diamond that has fifty-eight facets. It "reflects" a deep desire of the other person. And when one facet of a diamond reflects the light, in a sense the whole diamond shines. A plus sign will begin to appear on the forehead of that other person.

There is no ready-made list of value statements that can be applied to every situation in life. Much will depend upon our particular ministry and the people among whom we work. As we investigate the basic wishes of the human heart in the next chapter, the sources from which our value statements are derived will begin to emerge.

Chapter 4

HELPING PEOPLE EVOLVE: SURFACING AND EXPANDING THE BASIC WISHES OF THE HUMAN HEART

As cultural Christianity moves further into Stage Four, people in ministry tend to become more and more uneasy. Some of us may say, "We are building a house called ministry, but it keeps sinking into a quicksand called apathy." What we need is a new foundation. With the advent of Stage Four, the old foundations no longer suffice. In our eagerness to share Scripture, Christ, and the church with our people, we have neglected to see a whole new world open up under our feet. It is the world of the early stages of the evangelization process. It is a world where the assumptions of Stage Three cultural Christianity fall apart. It is where the game of ministry can be won or lost.

A Fatal Assumption about Religion

Matters that could be safely assumed in Stage Three cultural Christianity can no longer be taken for granted. In fact, these assumptions become fatal assumptions in Stage Four and do much to contribute to the quicksand which seems to be swallowing up our ministerial efforts. One of the most basic fatal assumptions is that religion is obviously good for everyone. We glibly offer people a chance to "get religion" from us. More and more the response those in ministry are hearing is something like this:

> I don't need religion. Oh, I'm not dropping out of it altogether. It's still handy for social transitions like wakes and weddings, or on Christmas and Easter. I just happen to think religion is not that important. I'm not against religion, mind you, but it's like a piece of costume jewelry. Some days you wear it; most days you don't.

Of course, people may not make this response to us directly. But they often make it indirectly by talking with their feet: They just don't show up! Young people are very sensitive to the present shift in cultural Christianity away from the blind acceptance of a group's religious values. This attitude is not limited to the young, however. Many of the not-so-young feel the same way and act accordingly—with negative footsteps. All of this leaves many in ministry with a massive self-image problem.

What is happening to us in ministry today is what happened to physicists early in the twentieth century. At that time the physicists were confident that they had a good grasp of their science. Of course, their confidence was based on the assumption that the atom was the smallest piece of matter. And then the bottom fell out of physics. But the collapse of one world opened up a whole new world of subatomic physics and led to a new golden age for that science.

What Is Religion?

The same challenge now faces us. If we put our own subatomic house in order, we may be pioneering a future golden age of ministry after this transition time is over. This leads us to the question: "Just what is religion?" I am not going to deal here in definitions but rather in working descriptions. A good working description of religion in Stage Three cultural Christianity would be adherence to the customs of the religious group into which we were born. In light of the Stage Four statement, that we rise or fall on the basis of our own basic convictions, it is becoming more difficult to persuade older adolescents and adults to accept a Stage Three type of religion. What we need now is a new working description of religion. Evangelization provides us with one.

One of the essential points in ministry today is the surfacing and expanding of the basic wishes of the human heart. The significant word here is "expanding." We in ministry have to help people stretch their minds and ask, "What do we really want out of existence?" We have to help them break down the cardboard boxes within their minds. We might say to a young woman, "You want to be a great movie actress but have no talent. No matter! Just include this desire on the list of the wishes of your heart. It will tell you something about yourself." People have to go right through their fantasy lives and come out on the other side.

Let us consider a concrete example of how this development takes place. The following can be done in many ways, but the dialogue form probably makes it easier for a reader to follow:

"I would like to be a famous television star."

"Why?"

"Well, millions of people would know me."

"Now, this is not a put-down. I just want to sharpen your thinking. Millions of people knew Hitler. So what?"

"Well, if millions of people knew me, I'll bet thousands would like me."

"Right. Now spin it out to its logical conclusion!"

"If millions knew me and thousands liked me, some of them would love me."

"You want to be loved—that's what you're really seeking!"

Our Four Basic Wishes

As this process unfolds, four basic wishes of the heart surface. The list is not final, and may be lengthened or shortened. These are the basic wishes that have emerged through this same process in various parts of the world. The four basic wishes of the heart are:

1. We want to love.
2. We want to be loved.
3. We want to share—in the sense that we want others to appre-

ciate our experiences and emotions, and we want to enter into the experiences and emotions of others. There is a cry for solidarity with God and others.

4. We want to blossom—we feel that there are all kinds of potentialities within us that we would like to see come to fruition. This includes the attainment of political, economic, social, and religious rights.

Naturally, how these basic wishes of the heart are fulfilled in concrete situations will vary according to our unique personality, the circumstances of life, and the inspiration of the Holy Spirit.

We should then be urged to take steps to attain these basic wishes of the heart. It quickly dawns on us that we cannot do it by ourselves. The only way *expanded* wishes of the human heart can be attained is by encountering a higher form of life—let us call it God—and by encountering other people. This then becomes our working description of religion. Religion is encountering God and others through whom we attain our basic wishes.

At this point we have a vested interest in religion. It is the way we progress toward attaining the basic wishes God has put in our hearts. It is something *we* want to do. It is not a task laid on us by our parents or those in ministry. Religion is now emanating from the inside out rather than from the outside in. What we are doing now is in accordance with the Stage Four cultural Christian mandate to rise or fall on our own basic convictions.

There is an amazing paradox here: The greater the basic wishes of our heart are, the more religious we become! The greater these wishes are, the more we feel the need to encounter God and others. That is why the really significant word here is "expanding." If we remain persons with very narrow wishes of the heart, which we feel we can attain by ourselves, then we remain trapped within ourselves. We remain self-ish and apathetic toward religion. If, on the other hand, we have greatly expanded the wishes of our heart, then we realize that the only way we can become self-full is by becoming full of God and others. As Saint Augustine says, "For the desire of your heart is itself your prayer. And if the desire is constant, so is your prayer."

In the account of Pentecost in the Acts of the Apostles (2:38), Peter calls upon the gathered crowd to repent (or in some translations, to reform). Unfortunately, neither of these English words catches the full nuances of the Greek original, the theme of *metanoia*. Both of these English words imply that this action is something we can do by ourselves. We can reform, we can repent, we can turn our hearts around simply by our own efforts. We might call this the spiritual weightlifter syndrome! Just as we can acquire muscles by lifting weights, so we can become more religious by means of our own efforts alone. We must remember that while what we do *is*, of course, important, we must open our hearts. Then if we are to attain the basic wishes of our hearts, we must depend on God and others to come into our hearts.

The surfacing and expanding of basic heart wishes, religion as encountering God and others in order to attain the basic heart wishes: this then is the matrix from which the value statements necessary to reach the encounter intuition are drawn.

It is from such humble (subatomic, if you will) origins that evangelization begins. And we must remember that in our ministry all our work at this subatomic level requires the greatest care. We are so eager to share Scripture, Christ, and the church with our people in this time of transition that we often neglect the new foundations that this time of transition demands. From this stage—preevangelization, if you will, in the sense that neither Scripture nor Christ have yet been mentioned—we and our people are now prepared to move on. These early experiences will shine down through the entire process and help us to recast Scripture, the rationale for the Incarnation, the church, and the fullness of time in terms of encounter experience. The great adventure will have begun.

Chapter 5

HELPING PEOPLE EVOLVE: THE EVOLUTIONARY MIND-SET

People cannot evolve without an evolutionary mind-set. Unfortunately, most cultural Christians still live in a static universe. They may admit that they are interested in "progress," but the kind of progress they mean is the perfecting of what already is. The present is seen as complete but imperfect. Progress then becomes a question of simply perfecting the present. Quantum leaps and basic changes are ruled out. What such people want is analagous to trying to turn an unruly twelve-year-old into a "nice" twelve-year-old while ruling out the possibility that the youth may one day mature into an adult.

The Key to the Future

Is there some key that will help us find a way both to understand what has happened in the past to bring about this situation and to discover a solution for the future? Very probably the key lies in the recesses of your mind as you read this page. The key or answer to this problem is *time*. We need better insights into time. It is paradoxical that time, which is always with us, becomes a very esoteric notion when we begin to investigate its meaning. Most of us prefer not to get involved in this problem. We cheerfully leave such speculations to the philosophers bent over their old parchments. Yet down through the years philosophical speculations regarding time have had immense implications for religion and life.

Plato's View of Time

As we begin to examine this key to modern ministry, we should keep in mind that what follows is presented in a most generic form. Many qualifying factors have been omitted in the interest of simplifying the thrust of our discussion. Long ago when Christianity first moved out of Palestine into the Mediterranean basin, the Christians of the early centuries began to seek a philosophical basis for the Christian message. They adopted the philosophy of the Greeks, in particular that of Plato. Plato had a very negative view of time. As far as he was concerned, the pure forms of all creatures exist "out there"—somewhere beyond our reach. For him, the reality we experience in our lives is just a poor imitation of these pure forms. We are living in a shadow world, and time is a mere moving through these shadows toward the real world of pure forms. As Plato's notion of time worked its way through the Christian message, heaven became the place of pure forms. Consequently this life was thought of as something to be gotten through as quickly as possible with as little fuss as possible. In the viewpoint of the early Christians, there is no sense in trying to evolve what is "here" on earth because it has no connection with what is "there" in heaven. The striving for perfection consists of finding the best way to go through "here" in order to be fully prepared for "there."

Thomas Aquinas's Quantum Leap

Then a radical theologian, Thomas Aquinas, tried to introduce a quantum leap in order to give our present passage through time a deeper meaning. He used the philosophy of Aristotle as the basis for his theological message. But since Islamic scholars were the source of the writings of Aristotle, church authorities at first viewed his works with a jaundiced eye. Aristotle had taken the pure forms of Plato and, under the new concept of "universals," placed them in all creation around us. In Aristotle's perspective time is important. What happens here on earth does have meaning.

With help from Aristotle, Thomas made a quantum leap, but Christianity was still in a static universe. "Here" took on a certain importance, but perfection consisted only in improving what is: an already complete universe. As Thomas's insights worked their way through the Christian message, the great emphasis was on good order.

Teilhard de Chardin's Views

Then came Pierre Teilhard de Chardin who announced that the whole universe is moving! It is moving, not just in a cyclic fashion as Thomas had said, but toward the Omega Point, the fullness of evolution. The universe is not yet complete. God's creation (in the full sense of the word) is still going on. He is gradually turning "here" into "there."

As a whole new sense of time appeared and gradually began working its way through the Christian message, there arose a quantum leap requiring dogma to develop, theology to be in process, church organization and its attendant structures to evolve, and our views of religion and life to evolve along with them. We have moved from a static universe to an evolving universe.

The shift from Fowler's Stage Three to Stage Four in Christianity is but a dramatic manifestation in our time of the ongoing work of the cosmic Christ, which is bringing the universe to the fullness of creation. We discover that the universe—including Christianity—is only twelve years old and has to evolve to maturity. And cultural Christians have to evolve along with the universe or perish.

This quantum leap concerning the importance of evolutionary time vaults us into the future. Teilhard's ideas, like Aquinas's in the past, are still viewed with a questioning eye by many. Today there are still some cultural Christians who deny the possibility of a quantum leap ever taking place in Christianity (in spite of the evidence of Aquinas's adventure). As long as that mind-set perdures, such persons have sentenced themselves to a static Stage Three brand of Christianity.

There are other cultural Christians who are not really against a quantum leap and an evolutionary mind-set, but neither are they fully in favor of this development. Such persons are confused. An explanation (in more pastoral and concrete terms, of course) of what has been presented so far in this chapter and the diagnosis offered in Chapters 1 and 2 might help to alleviate their anxieties, but often a gnawing fear will still persist.

The Challenge of Present-day Ministry

Quantum leap begets quantum leap. What we have to do is to move beyond Teilhard, as he was the first to tell us to do. I would propose a further quantum leap in the notion of time: a deeply pastoral examination of the fullness of time. It is not proposed that we in our present-day ministry will be able to carry out this quantum leap ourselves. Perhaps all we can hope to do is to put some fuel into the rocket that will achieve a successful quantum leap at some time in the future.

The challenge that lies before us in ministry today is to present to our people (and to ourselves) a deeper comprehension of the fullness of time. If we can in some way more fully understand the goal toward which the cosmic Christ is evolving the universe, then we shall have gone a long way toward allaying the fears of cultural Christians who are reluctant to join the great evolutionary adventure of our own day. Paradoxically, the more we can comprehend of the future's fullness of the Kingdom of God, the more successful will we be in our ministry today.

"Ah, but," you say, "who could even begin to comprehend the fullness of time? Didn't Paul give us an adequate presentation?" If Paul were to pay us in ministry a visit today, he would surely have cause to grumble. He might say to us:

> See what I did with the limited insights and tools available in my era! You have the advantage of almost two thousand years of Christian reflection on my work. You have brand-new evolutionary insights at your disposal. The work has just begun. Roll up your sleeves and get to it. And don't forget to rely on the Holy Spirit!

The challenge facing us is not just a study of what will occur in the ultimate future. It is also a call to what we and our people can experience in the immediate future. Once we posit an evolving universe, the fullness of time is not merely something relegated to the far distant future; we have the potential of experiencing a foretaste of it now. So our efforts will be aimed not solely at a study of the ultimate, but at a religious and life experience in the immediate future. We shall attempt in some small way to increase our comprehension of the ultimate future in order to deepen the experience of our encounter with God and others in the immediate future that starts today.

To sum up, we might symbolize the motion of time in the Christian message under Platonic influence as an arrow pointing to "up there."

In turn, we would symbolize the notion of time in the Christian message under Aristotelian influence, where we have motion in the universe (even though this notion remains one of good order in a static reality), as follows:

The quantum leap of recent times shows us a universe in the process of becoming, in the process of evolution:

Finally, the challenge for us in ministry today is to explore the ultimate future so as to provide an experiential foretaste of humanity's ultimate future in our own immediate future:

This is a call to put adventure and romance back into Christianity!

Chapter 6

THE ULTIMATE EVOLUTION: FORETASTE NOW

As we begin our investigation of the fullness of time—the ultimate evolution—we need to keep two things in mind. First, we have to be willing to stretch our minds and operate outside our usual categories. Although we seldom think of it, we actually exist in a prison—the prison of one time and one place. We have our existence only one second at a time. The previous second is already gone; the future second is yet to come. We are, quite literally, receiving only one drop of existence at a time. The same holds for place. Only one dot on the map indicates where we are. If we move, the former dot is gone. If we strive for another dot, we lose the present dot. If we are to begin to understand the interpersonal and evolutionary implications of the fullness of time, we have to be willing to break through our usual concepts or else remain trapped in our mini-minds and mini-hearts.

The second thing to keep in mind is that all that follows is tentative. All that follows is open to negotiation, qualification, change. Yet it might be well to remember that things that jar our mind-set on first hearing or reading often fall into place and synthesize if we give them time to crystallize in the back of our minds. After all, if we are undertaking this investigation in order to help our people evolve, we ourselves have to be willing to evolve.

The Fullness of Evolution

And so we ask ourselves: What is the fullness of evolution? It is ourselves with our resurrected bodies, alive in a radically changed universe that has become the site of these resurrected bodies. Not only that—the entire universe becomes the resurrected body of each of us. Our resurrected bodies are *coextensive* with the entire universe. "What difference does it make whether we have a large resurrected body or a small one?" some may ask. Ah, it makes a great difference. Consider for a moment the implications.

The entire universe has now become Christ's resurrected body. With the entire universe Christ encompasses and embraces all of us. By means of the entire universe Christ loves all of us. The entire universe is Christ. And yet, mystery of mysteries, the entire universe is also our resurrected bodies, and with this universe we embrace and love Christ. Each person's resurrected body is coextensive with the entire universe, and so with a universe that is alive and personalized we embrace each other in the ultimate union. If all this in its fullness were to happen to us now, we would lose our own uniqueness and personality, for we are as yet still very far down on the evolutionary ladder. It is only when we pass through the evolutionary transition called death-unto resurrection that we can experience the fullness of evolution without extinguishing our individuality. In fact, just the opposite will happen: Through our ultimate encounter with Christ and others, our own personality will be enhanced beyond our wildest dreams.

Our Ultimate Goal

What is the ultimate goal of religion and mysticism, of love and romance? It is to possess the beloved. It is to possess the beloved to such an extent that we become the beloved. And yet, mysteriously, we do not cease to exist so that the beloved in turn can become ourselves. This is what is at the central core of our hearts. It is what makes the universe move on. It is the fullness of time.

This is why we hug each other. This is why we partake of the Eucharist. We are striving to embrace the beloved. Each time we do so, we experience fulfillment and longing. We experience fulfillment because in some way the central desire of our heart has been met. We experience longing because we are looking forward to the ultimate embrace. The fullness of time will be the ultimate Mass act. Now a small amount of bread and wine becomes Christ's body; then the entire universe will become his body. The fullness of time will also become the ultimate marriage act. The act of embracing, of possessing and being possessed, will have attained its fullness.

By this interpenetration, in the fullness of time every desire for both individual fulfillment and union will have been achieved. An unending dynamic of encounter and personalization will take place. Greater encounter with Christ and others will beget greater personalization within us. Greater personalization within us will, in turn, beget even greater encounter with Christ and others.

Here we shall experience the epitome of mutual influence: the interflow of qualities. Christ's peace, wisdom, and ability to love will become ours. All our unique qualities will flow, as it were, into others and become their possession also. All their unique qualities of love, joy, and insight will become ours. Tangibility, warmth, attraction, and affinity will be the operative conditions. In this ultimate evolution of compenetrating-compenetrated reality, our ability to possess will expand to include the entire universe—a universe with a face, the face of Christ and the face of others.

This then will be the fullness of salvation. The expression "Jesus saves" often seems to smack of no more than tambourines, bass drums, and repentance from sin. The fullness of the salvific act of Christ, however, will encompass much more. All the minus factors of our present evolutionary struggle will have been destroyed: sin, first and foremost, but also sickness, pain, death, misunderstanding, confusion, boredom, and hurt. Not only will the minus factors be destroyed but in some mysterious way, by a rebound effect, they will also enhance our fullness of evolution. For example, Father Damien began his career as a handsome young man; he died with the ugliness of leprosy. In some mysterious way, his ugliness rebounds to further enhance his beauty in the fullness of evolution.

The fullness of salvation deals not only with the destruction and rebounding of the minus factors of our present life; it involves the positive factors of life as well. The basic wishes of the human heart—to love, to be loved, to share, to blossom out—will then be fulfilled beyond our wildest imagination. By the fullness of our encounter with Christ and others, by the resulting enhancement of personalization, the victory of Christ's salvific act will be completed.

The Trinity as a Prophecy

Unfortunately, our consideration of the Trinity is often viewed as a problem—a theological problem. But let us rather view the Trinity as a prophecy—a prophecy enlightening us on the fullness of evolution. Within the inner love-life of God there is an "I" and a "You." The "I" and "You" are constantly giving of self to the other in the fullness of love. We can call the "I" Father, and the "You" Son (Mother and Daughter, if you prefer). The giving-receiving, compenetrating-compenetrated encounter between the Father and Son is so intense and so personal that it is a person, the Holy Spirit. The whole process is so close and intimate that we have not three Gods but one God—God as "I" (the Father), God as "You" (the Son), and God as "We" (the Spirit)—within whom this love-life is taking place. Therein lies the mystery and the prophecy of the Trinity.

In like manner, the fullness of existence, the fullness of life, the fullness of love, the fullness of union—this entire experience of fullness—is trinitarian. The goal of all evolution under the hand of God, the goal of the entire universe, is to duplicate the inner love-life of the Trinity. It is to duplicate the giving-receiving, compenetrating encounter within God. Actually, the word "duplicate" does not encompass the full meaning of what the universe and life are striving to attain. The fullness of evolution is not merely the duplication of the inner love-life of the Trinity. Instead, it means being swept up into the inner love-life of the Trinity through the risen Christ.

God has been evolving this universe for approximately 15 billion years. Imagine watching the formation of our solar system about 5 billion years ago or the beginnings of life on our planet about 3.5 billion years ago. On the basis of what would have been present before our eyes at that time, who could imagine the present? Watching the coming together of atoms to form the sun and planets, or watching the coming together of molecules at the beginning of life forms, who could imagine the union and intimacy of two human beings in love?

Viewed from this perspective, the wonders that God has already brought about in the universe make words like "marvelous" and "spectacular" seem entirely inadequate. If so much has already happened in going from the past to the present, imagine the quantum leaps yet to come as the universe evolves to the ultimate future—a future of being completely swept up into the inner love-life of God.

And yet, the past and the present (which is soon to become the past) will not be lost. In some mysterious way the fullness of time will contain all previous time. All the good events in this transitional phase of our existence will be present to us for all eternity. Even all the bad events of this transitional time will be present to us for all eternity. But viewed from the context of the fullness of time, all the sin, shame, or suffering in them will have been defused by the providence of God. They will then be experienced in an ambiance of joy.

It is axiomatic to say that the greater includes the lesser. Although our ultimate resurrected bodies will be coextensive with the entire universe, there is no reason why they could not also manifest themselves in a more limited form, somewhat akin to what we might imagine our present bodily forms to be like if they were brought to a perfected state. We can imagine our ultimate resurrected bodies both in their greater state, which is coexistence with the universe, and in the lesser state of our present bodies perfected in the fullness of time. In some mysterious way both states will be possible simultaneously in the ultimate evolution. Our cosmic bodies will include our smaller bodies; ultimate time will include all previous time; ultimate creation will include all previous creation.

Again, another mystery: The fullness of time is not static, it is dynamic. It is perfection, and yet it moves on to even greater perfection. It is fullness, and yet we become capable of even greater fullness for all eternity! Why is this? Because the ultimate universe, even though it has been swept up into the inner love-life of the Trinity, continues for all eternity to plunge ever more dynamically into the depths of God's inner life, which is infinite. The operative conditions in the ultimate evolution are breakthrough, spontaneity, inventiveness, paroxysm, and ecstasy. Christianity is belief in the ultimate evolution: a personal universe plunging ever more deeply into a personal God.

The ultimate evolution does not pertain merely to the far distant future. We can have an experiential foretaste of all the ultimate adventure, love, and union that we have been investigating. This experience is available to us now in our immediate future— which begins today—if we are willing to leave our encounter intuition open to the value statements given above concerning the ultimate evolution. This means that we must be willing to expand the basic wishes of our hearts. We must be prepared to encounter Christ the Evolver with an evolutionary mind-set.

Christ the Evolver

The risen Christ who is our Evolver is transgeographical and transtemporal. Christ's resurrected body is now coextensive with the universe; the risen Christ is already in contact with the ultimate evolution. This jars the mini-minds and mini-hearts of those who occupy but one second of time and one dot of geography at any particular instant. We keep singing the praises of the risen Christ, and yet we keep trying to squeeze him into boxes of our making. Christ can never succeed in expanding us if we will not let him expand in our minds and hearts. Thus Christ the Evolver calls on us to experience him in a new way in the Easter-Pentecost process.

God has entered the human condition, and his presence among us culminates in Easter-Pentecost. In what does Easter-Pentecost ultimately consist? We are all aware of the various events—the appearances of the risen Christ and the descent of the Holy Spirit—mentioned in Scripture. But the question still remains: What ultimately is happening here? If we look at these events more closely, we can see that a number of people are being swept up into the inner love-life of God through the risen Christ. In this process they encounter God and others and so attain the basic wishes of their hearts.

This event did not take place only once. Rather it is a process that is still going on and will continue to go on unto the fullness of time. Easter-Pentecost is not simply a past event; it is an ongoing process carried out by a transtemporal and transgeographical risen Christ. We call this Easter-Pentecost process the church. This, ultimately, is what the church is. It is not merely a spiritual General Motors, one more organization, one more group on the face of the globe. Such a view of the church postulates a static mind-set. Church must be viewed with a dynamic or evolutionary mind-set; it must be seen as the central thrust of an evolving universe. It is to this that Christ the Evolver calls us, and it is in these terms that we in ministry must present church to others. It is in church as the Easter-Pentecost process that we hope to encounter Christ the Evolver and so experience a foretaste now of our ultimate evolution.

Chapter 7

IMPLICATIONS FOR JUSTICE AND PEACE

For centuries people have labored in a heroic fashion to allevi-ate the conditions of the poor, sick, elderly, underprivileged, and oppressed. In recent times, however, a quantum leap has taken place. We have begun to examine the sources, or causes, that initi-ate the deplorable conditions of the needy. Much systemic oppres-sion of an economic, political, social, and religious nature has been uncovered.

Uncovering systemic violence and making people aware of it are always difficult because the source of this violence is usually remote from its final disastrous effect. If someone were to go through a city and shoot dead a number of children, everyone would be immediately enraged by this Herod-like act. However, in the slums of some of the great cities of the world 50 percent of the children die before their eighth birthday, but little outrage is generated.

The Need to Uncover the Sources of Problems

There is a temptation to concentrate solely on alleviating the symptoms of any problem. This method of action is more direct, and somehow people seem to feel it is more Christian than to delve into economic, political, social, or religious systems. Yet we have come to realize that the only Christian thing to do is to un-

46

cover the sources of problems and then to strive resourcefully to bring about systemic change. In this matter the only way to have real success is not by putting a Band-Aid over a festering wound, but by having trust in actions on behalf of justice and peace that deal with both symptoms and sources.

What is the situation today? A small minority of cultural Christians are doing magnificent work in attacking the sources of justice and peace problems. The vast majority of cultural Christians, however, are not interested. They probably feel sorry for the poor and the oppressed, and donate funds to help lessen the symptoms of their plight. But most cultural Christians are not sufficiently concerned about justice and peace to deal with the sources of the problem. They simply do not see this call as one of the central concerns of Christian life. They see it as a peripheral role, a non-obligatory option. Clearly they have limited notions of what is essential to the Christian life.

As long as the majority of cultural Christians remain in Fowler's Stage Three, this situation will continue. Only if we in ministry can help people (and ourselves, of course) to evolve to the higher stages, can we hope to get more people involved in the vital justice and peace activity of uncovering and correcting initial causes. It is by employing the evangelization dynamics investigated in this book that we can help people reach the higher stages of faith ministry.

Let us now examine what happens vis-à-vis justice and peace when we move into Stage Four. As long as we remain in Stage Three, we are limited to the faith/life values of the immediate group into which by historical accident we were born. The result is that we are addicted to a kind of innate tribalism that fosters a maximum interest in our own immediate group as well as a minimal interest in the problems of persons outside our group. The authenticating and personalizing of our values that takes place in the transition to Stage Four will broaden our concern beyond its previous narrow limits. (Of course, if we can be helped to attain Stage Five or Six, the results listed below will be even better.)

People in Stage Four begin to think in terms of systemic change. As a result, they begin to consider dealing with the sources of economic, political, social, or religious abuses of human rights. Our Stage Four Christians are willing not only to go beyond their immediate group but are also willing to help former "outsiders" not only in terms of symptoms but also in terms of the source of those symptoms.

A great change likewise takes place in people whose rights and aspirations are systematically oppressed. It is surprisingly true that people in Stage Three who are suppressed by an economic, political, social, or religious establishment will still support the establishment. They will hope and pray that the symptoms of their problem will cease, but they will be reluctant to change the source of their problem, namely, the system. Why is this? Because the identity of people in Stage Three is so tied up with the status quo that it would be a form of psychic suicide for them to attack the establishment in which their existence is grounded. Only for people in Stage Four does the possibility of changing the system become a viable solution.

Power and the Violation of Human Rights

As mentioned in Chapter 2, a shift in the "virtues and vices" list occurs when a person enters Stage Four. Initiative, creativity, independence, criticism (evaluation leading to liberation)—all of which were viewed with suspicion in Stage Three—now are seen as necessary Christian virtues. Peace is no longer seen as a quiet maintenance of the status quo. From now on it will be apparent that there can be no true peace unless it is based on complete justice. Anger, in the sense of love disappointed, comes into play: People then may say, "We expected the upholding of certain values by the establishment, but they have failed to recognize them—and us!" Resistance to oppression, which always tries to wrap itself in the cloak of the rule of law, becomes necessary. Power is viewed with a critical eye. It is not that power is considered wrong in itself, but there arises a firm belief that if there is too much power in the hands of too few, if there is a lack of checks and balances, then human rights and aspirations generally are violated. Power is like fertilizer. Leave it all in one place and it produces an unpleasant smell; spread it out and it does good work.

As mentioned in Chapter 2, the person in Stage Four becomes

more community-minded. He or she becomes part of a fellowship seeking, among other things, Christian justice and peace.

Our Encounter with Christ the Evolver

In Stage Three the static mind-set prevails; "here" is this life, and "there" is heaven. Most religious aspirations and activities are centered on "there," and there is much less involvement in the matters of "here." As long as the static mind-set remains, the dichotomy of "here" and "there" also remains. In Stage Four this dichotomy begins to break down. There arises the possibility of an evolutionary mind-set as described in Chapter 5, as well as the possibility of a commitment to the ultimate evolution described in Chapter 6.

As a result of encounters with Christ the Evolver in the Easter-Pentecost process, such a person begins to realize that he or she is a co-evolver with Christ. Christ and the person must work together to perfect the universe. Within the Easter-Pentecost process, the Eucharist becomes an encounter with a trans-geographical and transsocial Christ, who unifies the lives of all people on earth. Systemic violence now affects all of us. One person's justice and peace problem is now everyone's problem. Activity on behalf of justice and peace is no longer an option. It is now part of the central core of Christian life.

Sociologists like to talk about "thick symbols." The theory goes something like this: An attentive elite (approximately 5 percent of a group) will respond to an appeal on the basis of the appeal itself. The vast majority of people, however, will only respond to an appeal if it is linked to their thick symbols, which are defined as meaningful signs belonging to the group that give to the members a sense of union and purpose.

Cultural Christianity at the present time is largely devoid of thick symbols. The thick symbols of the fifties and early sixties—the Latin liturgy, Baltimore Catechism, and similar presentations of the theology of the Council of Trent—are gone. Consequently there is now need of a new set of thick symbols. I propose that the new thick symbols be based not on a concrete book or language but on a series of search-and-encounter experiences, namely, the evangelization experiences that lead us to Stage Four and beyond. It is on this new type of thick symbol that the justice and peace appeal must be based if it is to be successful. (For an outline of search-and-encounter evangelization experiences see Chapter 8.)

Within the Church

In the Orient there is a saying: "At the foot of the lighthouse, there is darkness." The lighthouse passes on light to others, but remains partly in the dark itself. Unfortunately this saying applies also to a church that has succeeded in passing on an admirable message of justice and peace to all. With regard to the practice of the principles of justice and peace, however, certain aspects of the church leave much to be desired. (Within the church as the Easter-Pentecost process, there still lurks the church as a conglomerate, and there we encounter a maldistribution of power.)

Most of the power within the church is concentrated in the hands of an extremely small percentage of the church's membership. In the present structures this segment of the church tends to act as an oligarchy, making final decisions as to who will be selected to join the inner circle. In many instances this oligarchy merely duplicates itself by choosing new members who think the same as do those in the oligarchy. As a result, a structural inbreeding common to all oligarchies emerges. A single mind-set tends to both prevail and perpetuate itself.

The Imperial Model of the Church

By the Edict of Milan in 313 Constantine the Great told the early Christians that it was safe to come out of the catacombs. With the great wisdom of hindsight it now appears that they would have done better to remain underground. When they did, in fact, come into the open, there arose a great need for structure. Unfortunately, only one model was available at the time—the model of the Roman Empire, which was promptly adopted. This model is characterized by a highly centralized organization, a minimum of checks and balances, and the principle that the system is more important than its members.

Even if we were to concede that this was a suitable model for earlier times, as Christianity moves more and more into Stage Four we must likewise concede that the imperial model has become more and more counterproductive. If we persist in clinging to this model, we shall only slow down the transition of Christians to Stage Four, causing large numbers of people to leave the organized church.

The irony of this state of affairs is that there are several models of the church in Scripture. All of them have the essentials of the church, and yet the dynamics of each model varies greatly. The Palestinian churches put a rather heavy emphasis on structure and a vertical exercise of power. The Pauline churches were much more free-flowing, with a rather horizontal exercise of power in ministry. The Johannine churches were still more fluid. It is not now a question of adopting one of these scriptural models exactly as it existed centuries ago. The point is that the Easter-Pentecost process called the church is much more flexible than canon law and the prevailing mind-set could ever imagine. And so the cosmic Christ is warning us: "Evolve or perish!"

In all of this, it is not a question of "Power, power, who has the power?" Rather we have to understand that an overaccumulation of power—no matter where it is lodged in the present structure of the church—is counterproductive to the principles of justice and peace. For this accumulation of power undermines the justice and peace message of the church to the world. Besides, the imperial model tends to keep much of the church's membership in Stage Three and hence incapable of responding fully either to justice and peace or to the rest of the Christian vocation.

The Need for a New Model

A suggestion for the future can be summarized in three words:

> Converge
> Diverge
> Emerge

Let us imagine a group of people living on a ledge on the side of a mountain above a raging river. Let us call the people the church;

the ledge, the imperial model; the river, time. Gradually the river begins to rise and flood the ledge. The people gather, and their discussion goes something like this:

> We can no longer continue to *converge* on this ledge. We will now have to *diverge* and examine the series of paths leading up from the ledge. Some of the paths may lead nowhere, but we won't know that unless we try them. Other paths will, with the help of God, *emerge* onto a higher ledge where we can again *converge*.

We are in the position of the people on the ledge. Before we look for new paths, we need to keep in mind that even this higher ledge will not be our final convergence. For the river called time appears to be constantly rising. Therefore, we shall have to begin the process all over again. The imperial model is doomed, but the church as the Easter-Pentecost process will continue to evolve until the fullness of time.*

*The church in its evolutionary endeavors is now undergoing a tremendous emergence. In Appendix A, "Justice and Peace: The Rising Conscientization of the Church," this emergence is charted by an examination of the church's social documents since 1961. Unfortunately, the literary style of the documents often leaves much to be desired. Although the prose may not be vivid, the contents are indeed vivid and contain vivifying "good news." The aim of this appendix is not to document the complete social teaching of the church but rather, by culling pertinent passages from the documents, to enable readers to get a sense of the great emergence of justice and peace awareness that has taken place. The issue of justice and peace has moved from the periphery of Christian consciousness to become one of the central thrusts of the evolutionary phenomenon called Christianity.

Chapter 8

IMPLICATIONS FOR THE FUTURE CHRISTIAN COMMUNITY

In this chapter let us examine the channel out of which much of the emerging justice and peace action will flow: the future Christian community. Many exciting things are happening in the community of the church. As the structures of Stage Three crumble, new paths of community are being explored: prayer groups, service groups, outreach groups, lay leadership programs, renewal programs, and other programs that have their origins in the schools, college campuses, and parishes. Each of these groups, in turn, has its own particular thrust and characteristics. We might say that each has its own "personality." As a result, different groups will appeal to different people.

The Characteristics of Different Groups

Yet beneath this great variety of groups, each with its own special traits, lies a basis of common characteristics that are the hope of the future. These characteristics are worth examining because they will help constitute the future Christian community. Here is a list of the most noteworthy traits:

1. Most of these groups have a minimum of structure. The non-authoritarian, decentralized leadership operates in a horizontal rather than a vertical relationship to the members of the group.

2. When an exercise of power is necessary, checks and balances are present.

3. Because the groups are relatively new, they display an innate openness to new ideas.

4. Scripture is considered to be not only a source of religious information but also an essential element in giving life to the community. As the gospel is proclaimed in the community, the community itself becomes alive.

5. Prayer is personalized. There is an openness to a variety of prayer forms. Even if a particular prayer form does not appeal to an individual, he or she does not feel threatened when others use it.

6. Members of the group seek to go beyond the ritual aspects of the sacraments in an effort to reach the inner significance of these signs of grace.

7. A more personalized approach to Christ is present, and a capacity for joy is manifest.

8. Most of the groups are relatively small, or the units within the groups are small. As a result, all the members have a feeling of close association with other members of their group or subgroup.

In describing the feeling of love within such groups, we should note that one form of love, which we may call "in-love," quickly leads to another form, which we may call "out-love." In-love among members of a group builds up to such an extent that it must overflow as out-love to encompass persons outside the group. Paradoxically, the more intensified this out-love becomes, the greater is the in-love of the group's members for each other.

Most of the characteristics described above are found in the new groups, even though each group will maintain its own personality. Thus individual Christians eager for community are able to select a group that is best suited to their unique religious aspirations and to their own capacity for religious service.

Because we are investigating a wide variety of groups, what follows is necessarily presented in a very general way. If these conclusions are applied to a particular group, certain modifications and adaptations would, of course, be necessary.

To begin with, most of these new groups have an entrance period for new members. Generally, this is a well-thought-out process, finely tuned by usage over a fairly long period of time. It usually results in remarkable changes in the entrants. These initial processes should not be tampered with, for they reveal the unique personality of the particular group to those who are considering membership.

Once the initial entrance period is completed, many of the initial activities are repeated, generally in a more mature form. This mode of action usually works well for a period of time. Then, however, the law of diminishing returns may set in, and problems may begin to appear. New members may find that they have reached a plateau or hit a ceiling beyond which they cannot progress, no matter how often they repeat their initial experiences. At times this is the only difficulty. However, a series of negative elements may also appear. First and foremost would be discouragement, which might lead to a decision to leave the group. Other negative factors are the following:

1. A fundamentalist approach to Scripture;
2. An anti-intellectual attitude toward theological and philosophical problems;
3. An elitist attitude bordering on the pharisaical may develop toward all who are outside the particular group;
4. A tendency of some members of the group to dominate others;
5. A tendency for plurality of thought and attitudes to give way to uniformity;
6. An overemphasis on in-love within the group to the exclusion of out-love. The group may forget that after a certain degree of in-love has been attained, only the practice of out-love can further enhance the in-love.

Again, let us keep in mind that we are speaking in general terms. All these negative factors are rarely found in any one group. Perhaps it may happen that the only problem is the ceiling effect. Nevertheless, there is always a danger that the negative factors may appear and either severely damage the group or cause its dissolution.

To avoid this danger, there is need of a more concentrated application of the dynamics of evangelization and of the evangelization process. But the best place to uncover certain basic dynamics of evangelization is in a pure evangelization situation, namely, in

Asia or Africa. To attempt to do so in the United States, Europe, or Latin America would lead to difficulties because too many other factors would be present and would confuse the issue. Such factors are the heritage of cultural Christianity and traditional catechetics. No great discoveries can be made in a test tube already filled with chemicals from a previous experiment.

A New Process of Evangelization

In recent years an evangelization process originally developed in the Orient for use among non-Christians has been transculturated into a process for use among cultural Christians. This evangelization process is a series of search-and-encounter experiences by which we evolve to the higher stages of faith maturity. It consists of a series of prebaptismal experiences akin to those non-Christians go through on the way to Christianity, followed by the reexperience of our postbaptismal experiences in light of what has already occurred in this process. The following diagram and explanation attempt to depict this process.

10. Omega Point
9. Entering into a deeper spirituality
8. Conventional Christian activity
7. Baptism
6. Acceptance of God's entering the human condition
5. Realization that we cannot succeed alone (Scripture)
4. Encountering God and others (practice)
3. Encountering God and others (theory)
2. Searching step
1. Preliminary step

Step 1   Nothing is presupposed. We may well have highly negative attitudes toward God, ourselves, others, and religion. Perhaps God exists, perhaps he doesn't. If God exists, he may be more of a cosmic force than a personal God. Or he may be the God of the clouds—out there somewhere but with no real connection with our daily lives. There is also the possibility that we have a very poor self-image. We may be alienated from others. We may be surrounded by people, but dying of loneliness. Religion may be viewed as something for life's losers. It smacks of times past, of superstition, of moneymaking. It tends to manipulate people. Although some people may not be troubled with most of the above difficulties, the purpose of this stage is to make sure that even if one difficulty is present, it is acknowledged. There has been a tendency in cultural Christianity to suppress problems. In this preliminary stage nothing is taken for granted.

Step 2　A primal cry for more arises in our hearts. We may say, "There has to be more to life than we are experiencing!" We are not sure where we are heading, but the present condition is no longer acceptable. There is a gradual surfacing and expanding of the basic wishes of our heart.

Step 3　We begin to realize that the only way to attain our expanded basic wishes of the heart is to encounter a higher form of life (let us call it God) and to encounter others. There is an intellectual assent to this, but at this stage not much is done about it.

Step 4　We now make a real attempt to encounter God and others. For a while things go well, but there is a built-in trap. As seekers, we are relying solely on our own ability and insight. It is the spiritual weightlifter syndrome. Just as we can strengthen our muscles by lifting weights on our own, so now we are trying to attain encounter by our own efforts alone.

Step 5　Now a primal cry for help comes forth. We cry out, "God, whoever you are, wherever you are, help us. We cannot encounter you and others by our own efforts. We thought it would be easy, but it is proving exceedingly difficult to reach out, to be open, to love." This stage culminates in a new attitude toward Scripture, which is seen as God's reply to our primal call for help. However, here we are considering Scripture not so much as a source of religious information that tells about God, ourselves, and the meaning of life but as a causer of encounters. If we let ourselves go into the scriptural experience, this experience will gradually bring about encounters with God and others. This may not happen when we are reading or hearing Scripture, but may come later when we least expect it and are no longer trapped in our solitary efforts.

Step 6 Through Scripture as an encounter-causer we meet Christ the Encounter-Causer. Christ has entered the human condition in order to encounter each person with an intimacy beyond imagination, and he assists us to encounter others—again with an intimacy beyond belief. Christ's action culminates in the Easter-Pentecost event.

Step 7 Baptism is no longer viewed as a mere religious ritual by which one becomes a Lutheran, an Episcopalian, or a Catholic. Rather, it is seen as a deep encounter with the God who has entered the human condition as well as an encounter with the friends of Christ called the church.

Step 8 Easter-Pentecost is not just an event. It is a process that is still going on. It is a process by which we are swept up into the inner love-life of God through the risen Christ. There we encounter God and others, thus attaining the basic wishes of our heart. We call this process the church. The church ceases to be a mere static organization and becomes a dynamic adventure of process.

Step 9 This stage has infinite variety and infinite depth. How this stage unfolds will depend upon our own unique personality and on the Holy Spirit's leadership in the Christian adventure called life.

Step 10 This is the culmination of the Easter-Pentecost process—the ultimate evolution and fullness of time, as we discovered in Chapter 6.*

Earlier in this chapter we mentioned members of groups who reach a point beyond which they cannot seem to progress. Paradoxically, the way to break through the ceiling blocking Christian progress is for such persons to go back to the ultimate starting

---

*For a detailed account of the stages of evangelization mentioned above, see James DiGiacomo, S.J., and John Walsh, M.M., *The Encounter Series: The Longest Step, Meet the Lord* and *Going Together* plus three resource manuals. Full publication details are provided in Appendix B.

point in order to advance through the evangelization process described above. Just as an arrow has to be pulled backward in the bow before it can fly forward, so we as Christians have to undergo basic Christian experiences in order to break through the ceiling that has proved to be a barrier. Once the breakthrough is made, a whole new world of mature Christian experience is opened. As the positive factors above the ceiling increase, negative factors previously discussed will grow fewer.

In other words, let us assume that a Stage Three person enters a group seeking a new path to community. There the person undergoes initial experiences of a Stage Four quality. The person then hits the ceiling of progress located somewhere between Stage Three and Stage Four. The evangelization experience will then help this person to progress to Stage Four. (Another kind of breakthrough is also possible. Let us assume that the person has already attained Stage Four, but as a result of extreme polarization of his or her concepts. This polarization is the cause of the appearance of the negative factors listed earlier in this chapter. In this case the evangelization process may help such a group member attain a more balanced position in Stage Four. As a result of this balanced position, the person may go on to a whole new series of mature Christian experiences. His or her ability to advance to Stage Five is thereby increased.)

With the advent of an evangelization process within one of the groups described in this chapter, let us keep in mind the following principles:

1. The employment of evangelization does not mean scrapping the many activities and processes that have been used with success in the past. Rather we are urged to continue their use (with perhaps a finer tuning here or there) in our overall plan of evangelization.

2. An initiation process often brings about immediate results. But evangelization does not work that way. Its results are not immediate; they take time to surface. However, once the effects do surface, they tend to perdure in contrast to more immediate results that are sometimes short-lived.

We generally perceive progress to be charted like this:

Naturally, there are good days and bad days, so a progress line will have some breaks in it:

But this is still just a variation of the first progress line.

The progress line for evangelization, however, is different. It runs like this:

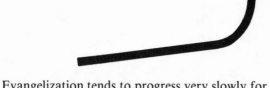

Evangelization tends to progress very slowly for some time, and then it takes off. Actually, this line is a more *natural* progress line. If we were to examine how God has caused the universe to progress over the years—whether in geological, biological, or human progress—we should find this development resembling the evangelization progress line. For example, humanity has been on this planet for untold centuries, but until 1900 the fastest we could travel was about 25 miles per hour. Now, a few years later, astronauts can leave the Earth for the moon at over 15,000 miles per hour!

3. It is well to resist the tendency to ask members of a group to give testimony as to what is happening to them *early* in the evangelization experience. Such testimony may have worked well in the initiation experiences of the group. In fact, testimony may have enhanced those experiences. Early in the evangelization ex-

perience, however, such testimony can be counterproductive. It is like pulling a little plant out of the ground every few hours to see if it is growing. The time for testimony will come as evangelization progresses.

4. Finally, members of a group should be informed that evangelization is not limited to the time when they meet together. It goes on twenty-four hours a day, seven days a week. The value statements of evangelization that we are exposed to during the meeting can result in encounters with Christ or with others at any time and in any place. Often such encounters occur when we least expect them. We must keep our minds and hearts open for surprises!

Chapter 9

THE SUCCESSFUL EVANGELIZER

Years ago a movie was made about General Erwin Rommel of the German Africa Korps in World War II. The film, entitled *The Desert Fox*, opens with a British commando raid on Rommel's headquarters on the Mediterranean coast. Leaving their submarine, the commandos paddle silently ashore in rubber rafts. They crawl to the headquarters building. Suddenly the commando leader blows his whistle, and chaos ensues. The commandos rush inside, guns go off, hand grenades explode, lights go out, furniture is smashed. The commando leader's whistle sounds a second time, and the commandos swiftly return to their submarine. Did they win or lose? No one is sure. All they know for certain is that there was chaos.

In this time of transition, many people in ministry often feel as if they have been on a commando raid. A whistle blows, they do their ministerial act, and then another whistle blows. Were they successful or not? No one is quite sure. In fact, they are not even sure what they were meant to do. The fog of war has descended upon ministry. No wonder so many people in ministry today have bruised self-images.

It is true that we who are in ministry do not expect to be successful all the time. After all, we are dealing with God's grace, human free will, and a modicum of talents on the part of ourselves as ministers. These things can never be programmed as in a computer. What we in ministry are seeking is an overview that will enable us to see above the smoke of the battle in order to understand what is taking place in ministerial methods during this time of transition.

An overview of ministerial methods is what we are seeking. Let us take Lonergan's four basic operations of the human psyche (described in Chapter 3), and examine three ways in which they have been handled: (1) by methods used in ministry prior to the mid-sixties; (2) by methods employed since the mid-sixties in a hurried reaction to changes occurring in Christianity; and (3) by new evangelization methods devised for today. Remember that we are dealing here with a general overview. Each part of what follows is negotiable and can be qualified by your own experiences as ministers.

WAYS OF MINISTRY

	Prior to the mid-sixties	Since the mid-sixties (in reaction to changes taking place)	New evangelization methods for today
Experiencing	Stage Three: God-centered	Stage Four: maximum	Stage Four: "natural" order of search-and-encounter experiences
Understanding	Information at a maximum level	minimum	Buildup by stages
Judging	"Pure" reason is appealed to	minimum	Coherence and motivation
Deciding	Adherence to the customs of the group	Stage Four: personal decision	Stage Four: personal decision, encounter intuition

Methods of Ministry Used
Prior to the Mid-sixties

In early childhood cultural Christians were introduced to a series of highly organized, uniform religious experiences that put heavy emphasis on ritual and were for the most part God-centered. Cultural Christians were expected to do as others did. The dominant note in this long-lasting era was an appeal to human understanding through the presentation of a coherent, all-encompassing body of religious information based on the theology of the Council of Trent.

Everything was in its place; there was a place for everything. Any theological idea or person that did not fit into the system was relegated to the limbo of nonidea or nonperson. Present also was an appeal to "pure" reason, which was believed to operate like a computer in splendid isolation from the rest of the person.

The basic thrust of ministry was formation through information that would maintain the cultural Christian in a continuing adherence to the customs of the religious group into which he or she was born.

Methods of Ministry Used
Since the Mid-sixties

As Stage Three of cultural Christianity ground to a halt in the mid-sixties, ministry was thrown into great confusion. What was to be the rule of action in a cultural Christianity that could no longer sustain itself by the automatic adherence of its members to the customs of the group? Great ministerial effort was now placed on providing cultural Christians with a series of personal religious experiences of a Stage Four type. These experiences were both God-centered and people-centered. Minimal effort was placed on an appeal to understanding and judgment. It was felt that if Christians underwent these personal religious experiences, they would then make a personal commitment of a Stage Four type to Christ and the church. At times the desired result was achieved; at times it was not. This mode of action was, on the whole, a good ministry, but it was not adequate for complete success.

New Evangelization Methods

Today's evangelization also puts a heavy emphasis on personal religious experiences. But these experiences unfold in a natural order—a supernatural order, if you will—based on prebaptismal search-and-encounter experiences of non-Christians on their way to Christianity. These, in turn, form the foundation for postbaptismal encounters. Because of the new foundation on which they are based, these postbaptismal encounters can be experienced with an intensity hitherto impossible. Not only does this natural order of encounter increase our depth of understanding and experience of Scripture, Christ, and the church, but it also provides a new integration. Until now, cultural Christianity has been plagued by a dichotomy between the good news concerning God and the good news concerning people. Until 1965 the former aspect of the good news was always stressed while the other merely tagged along. After 1965 we had about ten years of emphasis on people. Now the pendulum appears to be swinging back to God. Because evangelization begins at a subatomic level where the general dynamics of encounters are investigated, it would seem that God encounters and people encounters are now being integrated. Basically what we are saying is, "You have a love affair with Christ in the same way that you have a love affair with another person."

The appeal to human understanding is made through the content of the message of evangelization. This message is presented in a way that is different from that used in classical catechetics. Good pedagogy in classical catechetics demanded a logical unfolding of a whole theme at one time. While this was good for traditional catechetics, it is counterproductive for evangelization. Just as there is a natural order of search-and-encounter experiences, so there is a natural buildup by stages in the presentation of the content. Gradually a series of value statements and working descriptions is assembled. Taken all together, these value statements and working descriptions present an integrated Christian message.

In ministry today we are called upon to help our people make mature judgments on Christianity. This cannot be done unless we provide coherence and motivation. In Stage Three cultural Christianity, coherence was provided either by adhering to the Baltimore Catechism or by some more sophisticated presentation of theology as defined by the Council of Trent. No great emphasis on motivation was required because the system was self-perpetuating as new-born members grew up adhering to the religious customs of the group.

When Stage Three unwound in the mid-sixties, there was great emphasis on motivation. We in ministry were told to get people excited about Scripture, Christ, and the church. We were called upon to motivate the people. But the motivation was often a series of isolated urgings lacking coherence and content. As a result, ministerial efforts often succeeded for a short period of time in a hothouse atmosphere, but to a great extent lasting results were not obtained.

Because of this, a great cry has gone up: "Back to the basics!" It does not seem feasible to go back to the Baltimore Catechism or a variation thereof. The catechism provided coherence, but it was a static coherence that was viable only in a Stage Three cultural Christianity. Still those who cry, "Back to the basics!" have a point. We do need coherence, but it has to be a new type of coherence.

The new evangelization methods of today provide both motivation and the necessary new coherence. The motivation is easy to discover, for the process is filled with value statements calling people to an encounter with God and others. However, it is only when we go deeper into evangelization that the new type of coherence surfaces. It is the coming together of working descriptions.

In this book we have investigated religion as the encountering of God and others by which we attain the basic wishes of our hearts. We saw the church as the Easter-Pentecost process by which we are swept up into the inner love-life of God through the risen Christ. This led to an encounter with God and others, and so to the attainment of the basic wishes of our hearts. Within this Easter-Pentecost process, Scripture was seen as an encounter-causer that helped us to meet Christ and others. Christ, the center of the Easter-Pentecost process, entered the human condition to encounter us personally and to enable us to encounter others so that we could attain the basic wishes that God has put in our hearts.

We investigated the fullness of time as the culmination of this Easter-Pentecost process. The working descriptions of religion, church, the inner love-life of God (Trinity), Scripture, Incarnation, and the fullness of time all became of a piece. What resulted was not just some intellectual nicety formed by many descriptions fitting together, but a dynamic coherence for ongoing Christian reflection. If we want to plumb more deeply into any one of the themes, we can weigh it against the other themes. For example, if we want to enhance our appreciation of Scripture, we can weigh it against the working descriptions of religion, church, Trinity, Incarnation, the Easter-Pentecost process, and the fullness of time. Like a series of diamonds in a circle, each theme reflects and enhances the others.

What we have called the natural order of search-and-encounter *experiences*, the buildup by stages of *understanding* and *judgment* enhanced by coherence and motivation, all these culminate —under the grace of God—in a personal *decision* to have even greater love encounters with Christ and others. Especially in this decision phase we in ministry can facilitate these love encounters by keeping in mind the dynamics of encounter intuition (described in Chapter 3) that explain the ways in which we fall in love.

The above overview of ministerial methods will not solve all problems, but it will show the direction in which successful ministry is evolving. No one expects to score a touchdown on every play, but if we don't even know which way to run, we soon lose interest in the game. Once we know the direction in which the goal line lies, both the game and our self-image will improve.

•

As persons in ministry, we are *enablers*. By mastering the diagnosis of an evolving cultural Christianity, the dynamics of evangelization, and their implications, we are able to help others to evolve through encounter experiences. But we are more than that. We are *co-seekers*, for the basic wishes of our hearts also cry out for fulfillment. We too must go through these experiences along with those we serve.

May this book help bring adventure and romance to our people's lives—and to our lives as well!

I am the Alpha and the Omega, the First and the Last, the Beginning and the End. Let the one who hears answer, "Come!" Come, Lord Jesus! [Rev. 22:13,17,20].

NOTES

1. *Constitution of the Catholic Foreign Mission Society of America* (Maryknoll, New York: Maryknoll, 1980), Part I, Chapter I, Article 9, p. 4.

2. Philip Murnion, *Catholic Life in Yorkville* (New York: Archdiocese of New York, 1976).

3. James Fowler and Sam Keen, *Life Maps: Conversations on the Journey to Faith* (Minneapolis: Winston Press, 1978).

4. Ibid., pp. 25–39.

5. Ibid., pp. 25–29, 39–40.

6. Ibid., p. 40.

7. Ibid., pp. 24–33, 41.

8. Bernard Lonergan, *Method in Theology* (New York: Herder and Herder, 1972), pp. 3–55, 101–24.

Appendix A

JUSTICE AND PEACE: THE CONSCIENTIZATION OF THE CHURCH

We are in the process of a great "emergence" in the church: the sharpening of consciousness concerning the importance of justice and peace. Let us trace this mounting consciousness within the Catholic church from its beginnings to where it has become for the contemporary church a clarion call to Christian action.

In his encyclical *Mater et Magistra: Christianity and Social Progress* (May 15, 1961), John XXIII refers to the two major papal documents of social action of the past: *Rerum Novarum* (1891) and *Quadragesimo Anno* (1931). But in his work Pope John does far more than merely reemphasize the teachings of the past. In this document we see the beginnings of the spirit of *aggiornamento*—an opening to things new—which was to characterize Pope John's papacy to such a high degree.

Almost at the beginning of the encyclical Pope John says:

Hence, although Holy Church has the special task of sanctifying souls and of making them sharers of heavenly blessings, she is also solicitous for the requirements of men in their daily lives, not merely those relating to food and sustenance, but also to their comfort and advancement in various kinds of goods and in varying circumstances of time (3).[1]

This is the beginning of the breaking down of the old dualism between the spiritual and the material—a dualism that sometimes unconsciously, and at times consciously, placed the social apostolate in a second-class position in the ministry of the church.

The Pope then goes on to read the signs of the times, and to point out the ever-increasing complexity of social structures throughout the world:

> One of the principal characteristics of our time is the multiplication of social relationships, that is, a daily more complex interdependence of citizens (59).
>
> This tendency has given rise, especially in recent years, to organizations and institutes on both national and international levels, which relate to economic and social goals, to cultural and recreational activities, to athletics, to various professions, and to political affairs (60).

There is a consciousness here that all sections of life are becoming more and more interdependent and this awareness calls us to undertake a new and different analysis—an evaluation—of what is happening:

> Such an advance in social relationships definitely brings numerous services and advantages . . . (61).
>
> [But] methods are often used, procedures are adopted, and such an atmosphere develops wherein it becomes difficult for one to make decisions independently of outside influences, to do anything on his own initiative, to carry out in a fitting way his rights and duties, and to fully develop and perfect his personality. Will men perhaps then become automatons, and cease to be personally responsible, as these social relationships multiply more and more? It is a question which must be answered negatively (62).
>
> Actually, increased complexity of social life by no means results from a blind drive of natural forces . . . (63).
>
> . . . it is necessary that the public authorities have a correct understanding of the common good. This embraces the sum total of those conditions of social living, whereby men are enabled more fully and more readily to achieve their

own perfection . . . This they will do, only if individual members are treated as persons, and are encouraged to participate in the affairs of the group (65).

In the past most evaluation of structures has been done by those who profited most from maintaining the status quo within those structures—namely, the powerful. A new analysis is required. As Elizabeth Janeway states in *Powers of the Weak*:

Contemporary charts of the social world have been drawn up by the powerful without much regard for the ideas of the weak. They're based on events as seen by the powerful and interpreted by way of associations and connections that match the experience of the powerful. Our new discoveries are off the map.[2]

Even a quick analysis points out glaring inequalities. *Mater et Magistra* states that a particular country may be prosperous but much of the total wealth is in the hands of a few:

From this it follows that the economic prosperity of any people is to be assessed not so much from the sum total of goods and wealth possessed as from the distribution of goods according to norms of justice, so that everyone in the community can develop and perfect himself. For this, after all, is the end toward which all economic activity of a community is by nature ordered (74).[3]

Even if there is a just distribution of wealth and goods, there may be suppression of other human rights:

Consequently, if the organization and structure of economic life be such that the human dignity of workers is compromised, or their sense of responsibility is weakened or their freedom of action is removed, then we judge such an economic order to be unjust, even though it produces a vast amount of goods, whose distribution conforms to the norms of justice and equity (83).

As the globe grows smaller and interdependence among nations increases, the responsibility of the affluent nations becomes clearer:

> Therefore, the nations that enjoy a sufficiency and abundance of everything may not overlook the plight of other nations whose citizens experience such domestic problems that they are all but overcome by poverty and hunger, and are not able to enjoy basic human rights (157).

When one nation is helping another, care must be taken not to undermine the traditional customs that form the moral infrastructure of the receiving country. Even with the best of intentions it is possible for a highly developed nation to give material aid to another country in such a way as to cause psychic and moral harm to the receiving country:

> Nevertheless, while they pursue progress in science, technology, and economic life, they make so much of external benefits that for the most part they regard these as the highest goods of life. Accordingly, there are not lacking grave dangers in the help provided by more affluent nations for development of the poorer ones. For among the citizens of those latter nations, there is operative a general awareness of the higher values on which moral teaching rests—an awareness derived from ancient traditional custom which provides them with motivation (176).

The dichotomy of spiritual and material is breaking down. The person who dedicates self to promoting justice and peace is participating fully in Christ's ongoing redemptive work:

> . . . when they apply themselves to temporal affairs, their work in a way is a continuation of the labor of Jesus Christ Himself. . . . Human labor of this kind is so exalted and ennobled that it leads men engaged in it to spiritual perfection, and can likewise contribute to the diffusion and propagation of the fruits of Redemption to others. So also it results in the flow of that Gospel leaven, as it were, through the veins of civil society wherein we live and work (259).

Viewing this document many years after its first appearance, we may consider it unsophisticated. But let us not lose our perspective. It was a great breakthrough for its time and foreshadowed splendid things to come. As when one stands in the lobby of the Air and Space Museum in Washington, D.C., and looks at the Wright brothers' first airplane, its lack of sophistication is obvious, still one never fails to appreciate its significance.

•

In a second encyclical *Pacem in Terris: Peace on Earth* (April 11, 1963), Pope John carries his ideas further. Religion in the past often found itself the unwitting ally, and sometimes the willing ally, of the powerful in an unjust situation. As Marx rightly pointed out, organized religion often urged its adherents to look to the afterlife for redress and to suffer and endure the unjust present. But religion is a two-edged sword, and though it may have aided injustice at times in the past, it is no less able to turn its might against injustice. Janeway points out:

> Nevertheless, though access to the supernatural can seem to strengthen the powerful, faith can also help the weak . . . by keeping alive for them a sense of their personal significance and value and assuring them that they are seen and judged by a present God. This assurance can indeed keep the weak quiet and satisfied; but it doesn't always work that way. Access to the Godhead can also convince men and women to take issue with the powerful, to denounce the princes of this world. . . .[4]

In *Pacem in Terris* Pope John lists the rights of each human person:

> Beginning our discussion of the rights of man, we see that every man has the right to life, to bodily integrity, and to the means which are necessary and suitable for the proper development of life. These means are primarily food, clothing, shelter, rest, medical care, and finally the necessary social services . . . (11).[5]

The human person is also entitled to a juridical protection

of his rights, a protection that should be efficacious, impartial and in conformity with true norms of justice . . . (27).

The relations between the government and the governed are then set forth in terms of rights and duties. And it is clearly laid down that the paramount task assigned to government officials is that of recognizing, respecting, reconciling, protecting and promoting the rights and duties of citizens (77).

The dignity of the human person involves, moreover, the right to take an active part in public affairs and to contribute to the common good of the citizens . . . (26).

. . . Since women are becoming ever more conscious of their human dignity, they will not tolerate being treated as inanimate objects or mere instruments, but claim, both in domestic and in public life, the rights and duties that befit a human person (41).*

Naturally, Janeway tells us, those who stand to benefit most from an unjust state of affairs have their own plan:

Power, say the powerful, belongs to us because we do know how to use it. Our own definitions assure us that this is so, and as soon as we can once again persuade the weak to accept these obvious facts of life, they will see that power is not for them.[6]

The persuasion referred to here is often force cloaked in apparent legality. The Pope in two remarkable statements in *Pacem in Terris* forcefully attacks this apparent legality:

. . . For that reason, they are right in not easily yielding in obedience to an authority imposed by force, or to an authority in whose creation they had no part or to which they themselves did not decide to submit by conscious and free choice (138).[7]

---

*In many places in these documents one is perturbed by the masculine domination of both vocabulary and ideas. Yet paradoxically throughout the very documents themselves are the principles of human rights that will help to do away with these sexist attitudes.

Since the right to command is required by the moral order and has its source in God, it follows that if civil authorities legislate for, or allow, anything that is contrary to that order and therefore contrary to the will of God, neither the laws made nor the authorization granted can be binding on the consciences of the citizens, since "we must obey God rather than men" (51).

Moreover, human rights exist not only on a national, but also on an international scale:

Similarly, political communities may have reached different levels of culture, civilization or economic development. But that is not a sufficient reason for some to take unjust advantage of their superiority over others. Rather should they see in it an added motive for more serious commitment to the common cause of social progress (88).

It is vitally important, therefore, that the wealthier states, in providing varied forms of assistance to the poorer, should respect the moral heritage and ethnic characteristics peculiar to each, and also that they should avoid any intention of political domination . . . (125).

It is often true that even if nations have the desire to act in accordance with the two statements above, much of the potential for doing this is eaten away by the cancer of the arms race:

On the other hand, it is with deep sorrow that We note the enormous stocks of armaments that have been and still are being made in the more economically developed countries with a vast outlay of intellectual and economic resources. And so it happens that, while the people of these countries are loaded with heavy burdens, other countries as a result are deprived of the collaboration they need in order to make economic and social progress (109).

On an average, the money required to arm and train one soldier would be enough to educate 80 children. There are approximately 22 million soldiers and 22 million teachers in the world. Sixty times more money is spent on soldiers than on teachers. Each year approximately 400 billion dollars is spent on arms. This amount is equivalent to the entire annual income of the poorer half of the human race.

As interdependence and its accompanying responsibility grow throughout the world, Pope John presents us with the following challenge:

At the present time no political community is able to pursue its own interests and develop itself in isolation, because its prosperity and development are both a reflection and a component part of the prosperity and development of all the political communities (131).

There is an immense task incumbent on all men of good will, namely, the task of restoring the relations of the human family in truth, in justice, in love and in freedom—the relations between individual human beings; between citizens and their respective political communities; between political communities themselves; between individuals, families, intermediate associations and political communities on the one hand, and the world community on the other (163).

•

Mater et Magistra and *Pacem in Terris* laid the groundwork for *Gaudium et Spes: Pastoral Constitution on the Church in the Modern World* (Second Vatican Council, December 7, 1965). This document has become the foundation of the justice and peace apostolate. At the outset the document states:

The joys and the hopes, the griefs and the anxieties of men of this age, especially those who are poor or in any way afflicted, these too are the joys and hopes, the griefs and anxieties of the followers of Christ . . . (1).

Therefore, the Council focuses its attention on the world of men, the whole human family along with the sum of those realities in the midst of which that family lives (3).[8]

Reflection on the present situation in the world then begins to surface:

> . . . Today, the human race is passing through a new stage of its history. Profound and rapid changes are spreading by degrees around the whole world. . . . As happens in any crisis of growth, this transformation has brought serious difficulties in its wake. . . . Never has the human race enjoyed such an abundance of wealth, resources, and economic power. Yet a huge proportion of the world's citizens is still tormented by hunger and poverty. . . . Never before today has man been so keenly aware of freedom, yet at the same time, new forms of social and psychological slavery make their appearance . . . (4).

> A change in attitudes and in human structures frequently calls accepted values into question. . . . The institutions, laws, and modes of thinking and feeling as handed down from previous generations do not always seem to be well adapted to the contemporary state of affairs. . . . As a consequence, many people are shaken (7).

This view of the world has become a basis for the justice and peace movement:

> . . . History itself speeds along on so rapid a course that an individual person can scarcely keep abreast of it. The destiny of the human community has become all of a piece, where once the various groups of men had a kind of private history of their own. Thus, the human race has passed from a rather *static* concept of reality to a more *dynamic, evolutionary* one. In consequence, there has arisen a new series of problems, a series as important as can be, calling for new efforts of analysis and synthesis (5) [Italics added].

The above passage indicates the beginnings of a shift in the mind-set of the church. The static approach (with its emphasis on preserving the present state of affairs, and its preference for evading a question rather than taking the chance of making mistakes) is no longer viable. As we saw in Chapter 5 of this book, there is a necessity for an evolutionary mind-set. The evolutionary approach (with its emphasis on the willingness to evaluate, to probe, to reach out, to think new thoughts, to change, to risk adventure) provides the openness that is necessary for successful justice and peace ministry.

The static mind-set premised that the individual group or nation could hope to succeed in splendid isolation. The evolutionary mind-set takes the opposite approach:

Every day human interdependence grows more tightly drawn and spreads by degrees over the whole world. As a result the common good, that is, the sum of those conditions of social life which allow social groups and their individual members relatively thorough and ready access to their own fulfillment, today takes on an increasingly universal complexion and consequently involves rights and duties with respect to the whole human race . . . (26).

It is Christ in his continuing work upon earth who is at the source of the ever-increasing interdependence of people. And it is Christ who is bringing forth the ever-growing cry within the peoples of the world for human rights and human progress:

. . . Appointed Lord by His resurrection and given plenary power in heaven and on earth, Christ is now at work in the hearts of men through the energy of His Spirit. He arouses not only a desire for the age to come, but, by that very fact, He animates, purifies, and strengthens those noble longings too by which the human family strives to make its life more human and to render the whole earth submissive to this goal . . . (38).

We await the ultimate evolution that is to come:

. . . we are taught that God is preparing a new dwelling place and a new earth where justice will abide, and whose blessedness will answer and surpass all longings for peace which spring up in the human heart . . . (39).

Yet, as we saw in Chapter 6 of this book, we are to experience now a foretaste of this just and peaceful state. But this foretaste will be possible only if we labor with Christ to bring it about:

> . . . the expectation of a new earth must not weaken but rather stimulate our concern for cultivating this one. For here grows the body of a new human family, a body which even now is able to give some kind of foreshadowing of the new age (39).

Christ, of course, is the prime architect of both the ultimate evolution and our foretaste of it now. We, however, are co-evolvers in Christ's ongoing work. We are being called upon more and more to shoulder our share of the task. Hence, there is an ever increasing value to all human activity in general and to justice and peace undertakings in particular:

> Thus, far from thinking that works produced by man's own talent and energy are in opposition to God's power and that the rational creature exists as a kind of rival to the Creator, Christians are convinced that the triumphs of the human race are a sign of God's greatness and the flowering of His own mysterious design. For the greater man's power becomes, the farther his individual and community responsibility extends. Hence it is clear that men are not deterred by the Christian message from building up the world, or impelled to neglect the welfare of their fellows. They are, rather, more stringently bound to do these very things (34).

All humanity is called to participate in the evolutionary task and so the church expresses its willingness to dialogue with the entire world—not only to speak, but to listen; not only to give, but to receive:

> Though mankind today is struck with wonder at its own discoveries and its power, it often raises anxious questions about the current trend of the world, about the place and role of man in the universe, about the meaning of his individual and collective strivings, and about the ultimate des-

tiny of reality and of humanity. Hence, . . . this Council can provide no more eloquent proof of its solidarity with the entire human family. . . than by engaging with it in conversation about these various problems (3).

The church looks forward to helping all people to discover the basic truths about themselves:

Modern man is on the road to a more thorough development of his own personality, and to a growing discovery and vindication of his own rights. Since it has been entrusted to the Church to reveal the mystery of God, who is the ultimate goal of man, she opens up to man at the same time the meaning of his own existence, that is, the innermost truth about himself . . . (41).

To carry out such a task, the Church has always had the duty of scrutinizing the signs of the times and of interpreting them in the light of the gospel . . . (4).

At the same time the church must acknowledge the past riches received and the future riches awaited:

Just as it is in the world's interest to acknowledge the Church as a historical reality, and to recognize her good influence, so the Church herself knows how richly she has profited by the history and development of humanity.

Thanks to the experience of past ages, the progress of the sciences, and the treasures hidden in the various forms of human culture, the nature of man himself is more clearly revealed and new roads to truth are opened . . . (44).

And so the church in conjunction with the wisdom of others begins to probe further into certain problems of special import. Let us examine a few of the highlights of this investigation.

Culture provides the matrix of our human endeavors. Yet throughout the world this all-important base of human activity is rapidly changing:

The living conditions of modern man have been so profoundly changed in their social and cultural dimensions, that we can speak of a new age in human history. . . (54).

In every group or nation, there is an ever-increasing number of men and women who are conscious that they themselves are the artisans and the authors of the culture of their community. Throughout the world there is a similar growth in the combined sense of independence and responsibility. Such a development is of paramount importance for the spiritual and moral maturity of the human race . . . (55).

In the light of these changes certain principles must be kept in mind:

. . . the human spirit must be cultivated in such a way that there results a growth in its ability to wonder, to understand, to contemplate, to make personal judgments, and to develop a religious, moral, and social sense . . . (59).

Because it flows immediately from man's spiritual and social nature, culture has constant need of a just freedom if it is to develop . . . (59).

. . . By these decisions universal recognition and implementation should be given to the right of all men to a human and civic culture favorable to personal dignity and free from any discrimination on the grounds of race, sex, nationality, religious, or social conditions . . . (60).

. . . For in truth it must still be regretted that fundamental rights are not yet being universally honored. Such is the case of a woman who is denied the right and freedom to choose a husband, to embrace a state of life, or to acquire an education or cultural benefits equal to those recognized for men . . . (29).

Likewise, in the matter of economics it must be kept in mind that economics serves the human person and not the other way around:

In the socio-economic realm, too, the dignity and total vocation of the human person must be honored and advanced along with the welfare of society as a whole. For man is the source, the center, and the purpose of all socio-economic life. . . .

Again, we are at a moment in history when the development of economic life could diminish social inequalities if that development were guided and coordinated in a reasonable and human way. Yet all too often it serves only to intensify the inequalities. In some places it even results in a decline in the social status of the weak and in contempt for the poor. . . (63).

Among countless examples of inequality, let us consider one: Caracas, Venezuela. The center of Caracas is for the most part made up either of buildings of historical antiquity or modern edifices that reflect great prosperity. But as one looks to the surrounding hills, the plight of the unfortunate glares out. The higher one looks up the hills, the poorer the shacks become. The inequality is strikingly evident, unlike many places both here and abroad where poverty is hidden in the slums of the inner city or in the temporary quarters of migrant farmers far out in the countryside, to be discovered only when searched out.

All this leads us to conclude that if we want to further the evolution of the Kingdom of God, we must further economic development:

Christians who take an active part in modern socio-economic development and defend justice and charity should be convinced that they can make a great contribution to the prosperity of mankind and the peace of the world. . . .

Whoever in obedience to Christ seeks first the kingdom of God will as a consequence receive a stronger and purer love *for helping all his brothers* and *for perfecting the work of justice* under the inspiration of charity (72) [Italics added].

In this connection it should be remembered that it is not enough to help people with merely transient aid. We must help people in such a way that gradually they can begin to have a greater voice in and control over their own destiny. Empowerment is the key:

Economic development must be kept under the control of mankind. It must not be left to the sole judgment of a few men or groups possessing excessive economic power, or of the political community alone, or of certain especially pow-

erful nations. It is proper, on the contrary, that at every level
the largest possible number of people have an active share in
directing that development . . . (65).

As in culture and economics, so also in politics, great changes
are taking place:

> Our times have witnessed profound changes too in the insti-
> tutions of peoples and in the ways that peoples are joined
> together. . . .
> Men are voicing disapproval of any kind of government
> which blocks civil or religious liberty, multiplies the victims
> of ambition and political crimes, and wrenches the exercise
> of authority from pursuing the common good to serving
> the advantage of a certain faction or of the rulers them-
> selves . . . (73).

But injustice can be attacked, the empowerment of others can
be furthered, only if we are willing to enter more deeply into the
political process:

> . . . Let all Christians appreciate their special and personal
> vocation in the political community. This vocation requires
> that they give conspicuous example of devotion to the sense
> of duty and of service to the advancement of the common
> good . . . (75).

For there can be no true peace without justice:

> Peace is not merely the absence of war. . . . Instead it is
> rightly and appropriately called "an enterprise of justice"
> (Is. 32:7). Peace results from that harmony built into hu-
> man society by its divine Founder, and actualized by men as
> they thirst after ever greater justice . . . (78).

Gaudium et Spes also calls for an open-ended approach and
respect for diversity:

> . . . Undeniably this conciliar program is but a general one.
> . . . The program will have to be further pursued and ampli-

fied, since it often deals with matters in a constant state of development . . . (91).

Such a mission requires . . . that we foster within the Church herself mutual esteem, reverence, and harmony, through the full recognition of lawful diversity. . . (92).

And it concludes with a ringing challenge:

. . . Therefore, holding faithfully to the gospel and benefiting from its resources, and united with every man who loves and practices justice, Christians have shouldered a gigantic task demanding fulfillment in this world. . . .

Not everyone who cries, "Lord, Lord," will enter into the kingdom of heaven, but those who do the Father's will and take a strong grip on the work at hand . . . (93).

•

Populorum Progessio: On the Development of Peoples (March 26, 1967), the encyclical of Paul VI, continues the work of Vatican II. This document presents the goal of human development:

Freedom from misery, the greater assurance of finding subsistence, health and fixed employment; an increased share of responsibility without oppression of any kind and in security from situations that do violence to their dignity as men; better education—in brief, *to seek to do more, know more and have more in order to be more*: that is what men aspire to now when a greater number of them are condemned to live in conditions that make this lawful desire illusory. . . (6) [Italics added].[9]

Bold undertakings with emphasis on empowerment are necessary to attain the goal of human development and liberation:

. . . local and individual undertakings are no longer enough. The present situation of the world demands concerted action based on a clear vision of all economic, social, cultural, and spiritual aspects . . . (13).

We want to be clearly understood: the present situation must be faced with courage and the injustices linked with it must be fought against and overcome. Development demands bold transformations, innovations that go deep . . . (32).

. . . It is not just a matter of eliminating hunger, nor even of reducing poverty. The struggle against destitution, though urgent and necessary, is not enough. It is a question, rather, of building a world where every man, no matter what his race, religion or nationality, can live a fully human life, *freed from servitude imposed on him by other men* or by natural forces over which he has not sufficient control . . . (47) [Italics added].

. . . There is also the scandal of glaring inequalities not merely in the enjoyment of possessions *but even more in the exercise of power.* While a small restricted group enjoys a refined civilization in certain regions, the remainder of the population, poor and scattered, "is *deprived of nearly all possibility of personal initiative and of responsibility,* and oftentimes even its living and working conditions are unworthy of the human person" (9) [Italics added].

Those who exercise power in an unjust situation will, for the most part, allow people in ministry to labor to alleviate suffering and want. They will usually not interfere in such attempts as long as those in ministry merely deal with the symptoms of the problem. The conflict comes when those in ministry turn to the source of the problem, namely, a maldistribution of power in some form: economic, political, social, or religious. Once the work of ministry turns to identifying the source of the problem, opposition arises. Once the attempt is made to bring about structural changes (the empowerment of the powerless), the opposition intensifies. Deal with the symptoms of a problem and be prepared to be praised. Deal with the source of a problem and be prepared to be condemned as disloyal, unfaithful, a troublemaker, or a supporter of radicals.

If we expect *conflict* from the powerful, we can also expect *challenge* from the weak. As long as the weak remain in Fowler's Stage Three condition, they will gladly accept alleviation of the symptoms of a problem, but they will be reluctant to accept structural or systemic change. Why is this? Because in Stage Three one accepts the status quo in a precritical (without evaluation) manner. In fact, one's personal identity is so closely connected with the status quo that it would border on psychic annihilation to attack the structures within which one exists.

Over and above this, the powerful are constantly sending a message to the weak that they (the powerful) are in some way destined to rule. Janeway comments on this point:

> If most of us were asked about our capacity to command the course of events, we would have to admit that we are both dubious of success and a bit afraid to try. But we assume that this is just what the powerful *can* do, for they assure us that they are doing it. Therefore, *they must be different from us,* they must have an inborn ability we lack, they must be intended and specially fitted by nature, or by some divinity, to do what we can't—that is, to wield power. . . .[10]

The weak will continue to reject systemic change until they are helped to evolve to Stage Four where the critical (evaluation) process begins. It goes without saying that a Stage Five person is even more suited to systemic change, but a Stage Four outlook is an indispensable condition for undergoing structural change.

•

Paul VI in his encyclical *Octogesima Adveniens: The Eightieth Anniversary of "Rerum Novarum"* (May 14, 1971) provides us with a very interesting insight into Marxism:

> For some, Marxism remains essentially the active practice of class struggle. Experiencing the ever present and continually renewed force of the relationships of domination and exploitation among men, they reduce Marxism to no more than a struggle—at times with no other purpose—to be pursued and even stirred up in permanent fashion. For others, it is first and foremost the collective exercise of political and economic power under the direction of a single party, which

would be the sole expression and guarantee of the welfare of all, and would deprive individuals and other groups of any possibility of initiative and choice. At a third level, Marxism, whether in power or not, is viewed as a socialist ideology based on historical materialism and the denial of everything transcendent . . . (33).[11]

But then the document adds a most important distinction:

At other times, finally, it presents itself in a more attenuated form, one also more attractive to the modern mind: as a scientific activity, as a rigorous method of examining social and political reality, and as the rational link, tested by history, between theoretical knowledge and the practice of revolutionary transformation. Although this type of analysis gives a privileged position to certain aspects of reality to the detriment of the rest, and interprets them in the light of its ideology, *it nevertheless furnishes some people not only with a working tool but also a certitude preliminary to action: the claim to decipher in a scientific manner the mainsprings of the evolution of society* . . . (33) [Italics added].

In examining the *Pastoral Constitution on the Church in the Modern World,* we saw the church's willingness to dialogue with all of humanity. While most people will accept dialogue in principle, for many it becomes "duologue" in practice. Both parties speak but neither listens: "The other party is completely wrong and has nothing to tell me." Dialogue, though not accepting the other's position uncritically, does encompass a willingness to learn, to be open to insight, to find common ground.

Octogesima Adveniens shows a willingness to use certain Marxist procedures: the structural analysis of systems of power, the dynamics of societal change, the use of praxis as an ongoing dialectical exchange between theory and practice. Unfortunately, when most people hear the word "Marxism," a "duologue" mentality is set up. Otherwise sophisticated people, who can be very discerning in accepting or rejecting certain parts of a whole, become very simplistic about Marxism and reject everything out of hand. This document challenges us to act differently.

•

Still another recent document, *Evangelii Nuntiandi: On Evangelization in the Modern World* (December 8, 1975), of Paul VI remains to be considered. The central theme is presented thus:

> The witness that the Lord gives of himself and that Saint Luke gathered together in his Gospel—"I must proclaim the Good News of the kingdom of God"—without doubt has enormous consequences, for it sums up the whole mission of Jesus: "that is what I was sent to do" (6).[12]

But the full meaning of the theme becomes clear only later:

> These words take on their full significance if one links them with the previous verses, in which Christ has just applied to himself the words of the Prophet Isaiah: "The Spirit of the Lord has been given to me, for he has anointed me. He has sent me to bring the good news to the poor" (6).

The church recognizes this as its central mission:

> We wish to confirm once more that the task of evangelizing all people constitutes the essential mission of the Church. It is a task and mission which the vast and profound changes of present-day society make all the more urgent. Evangelizing is in fact the grace and vocation proper to the Church, her deepest identity (14).

However, if we are to appreciate the full meaning of evangelization, we must be open to its many facets, for evangelization is a complicated procedure that involves many components.

> Evangelization, as we have said, is a complex process made up of varied elements: the renewal of humanity, witness, explicit proclamation, inner adherence, entry into the community, acceptance of signs, apostolic initiative. These elements may appear to be contradictory, indeed mutually ex-

clusive. In fact they are complementary and mutually enriching (24).

But the full implications of evangelization become plain only when it is viewed in terms of human development, liberation, justice, and peace:

> Peoples, as we know, are engaged with all their energy in the effort and struggle to overcome everything which condemns them to remain on the margin of life: famine, chronic disease, illiteracy, poverty, injustices in international relations and especially in commercial exchanges, situations of economic and cultural neo-colonialism sometimes as cruel as the old political colonialism. The Church, as the Bishops repeated, has the duty to proclaim the liberation of millions of human beings, many of whom are her own children—the duty of assisting the birth of this liberation, of giving witness to it, of ensuring that it is complete (30).
>
> Between evangelization and human advancement—development and liberation—there are in fact profound links. . . . They include links of the eminently evangelical order, which is that of charity: how in fact can one proclaim the new commandment (of love) without promoting in justice and in peace the true, authentic advancement of man (31)?
>
> Hence, when preaching liberation and associating herself with those who are working and suffering for it, the Church is certainly not willing to restrict her mission only to the religious field and disassociate herself from man's temporal problems (34).
>
> The Church considers it to be undoubtedly important to build up structures which are more human, more just, more respectful of the rights of the person and less oppressive and less enslaving . . .(36).

What we observe here is a further dissolution of the body-soul dichotomy that has plagued ministry for so long. Body-soul may be a good *distinction* for use in certain forms of theology, but unfortunately it has often become a *dichotomy* when transferred to actual ministry: sacred versus secular, eternal versus time, spiritual versus material. Actually, with the dissolution of a body-soul dichotomy, we are closer to the mind-set of Christ and Paul as found in Scripture. Christ and Paul as Semites had a Semitic view of the human person. They considered a person from the viewpoints of *basar, nephesh* and *ruah* (*soma, psyche,* and *pneuma.*) These were considered not so much as "parts" of a person (body, soul) but rather as three aspects for viewing the *one whole totality* that is a person. For Christ and Paul there was no dichotomy. The person is a totality: an embodied person, a personalized body, a body-person. And one ministers to the whole person. The church is in the process of reaffirming this most important scriptural insight when it states that human development, liberation, justice, and peace are *integral* parts of the ministry of evangelization.

As we undertake the work of evangelization, we are reminded to evangelize ourselves:

The Church is an evangelizer, but she begins by being evangelized herself. She is the community of believers, the community of hope lived and communicated, the community of brotherly love; and she needs to listen unceasingly to what she must believe, to her reasons for hoping, to the new commandment of love (15).

And finally there is the need for the testimony of concrete social action:

The Church is trying more and more to encourage large numbers of Christians to devote themselves to the liberation of men. She is providing these Christian "liberators" with the inspiration of faith, the motivation of fraternal love, a social teaching which the true Christian cannot ignore and which he must make the foundation of his wisdom and of his experience *in order to translate it concretely into forms of action, participation and commitment.* . . . The Church strives always to insert the Christian struggle for liberation into the universal plan of salvation which she herself proclaims (38) [Italics added].

•

"To Live in Christ Jesus" (U.S. Bishops' Pastoral, November 1976) takes up many of the themes already discussed in the above-cited documents and particularizes them for the U.S. situation, advising us:

Christ tells us something new about God, about love, and about ourselves. His commandment to love is new not simply because of the scope and unselfishness of the love involved, but because it calls us to love with a divine love called charity, as the Father, Son and Spirit do. This call carries with it the inner gift of their life and the power of their love. . . .

All of us seek happiness: life, peace, joy, a wholeness and wholesomeness of being. . . . We rejoice in friends, in being alive, in being treated as persons rather than things, in knowing the truth. In this we are rejoicing in being ourselves, images of God called to be His children. Truth and life, love and peace, justice and friendship go into what it means to be human.[13]

Animated by our participation in the inner love life of God we strive to carry out Christ's mandate to aid our neighbor in attaining this human fullness:

As followers of Jesus we are called to express love of neighbor in deeds which help others realize their human potential. This, too, has consequences for the structures of society. Law and public policy do not substitute for the personal acts by which we express love of neighbor; but love of neighbor impels us to work for laws, policies and social structures which foster human goods in the lives of all persons.[14]

Although we should aid all people in attaining human fullness, some people have been particularly discriminated against and deserve our special help:

As society has grown more sensitive to some new or newly recognized issues and needs . . . the movement to claim equal rights for women makes it clear that they must now assume their rightful place as partners in family, institutional, and public life. The development of these roles can and should be enriching for both men and women. . . .

There is much to be done in the Church in identifying appropriate ways of recognizing women's equality and dignity. . . .

Racial antagonism and discrimination are among the most persistent and destructive evils in our nation. Those victims of discrimination of whom we are most conscious are Hispanic Americans, Black Americans, and American Indians. . . .

An injustice to which we have frequently drawn attention is the systematic exploitation of agricultural workers, many of them migrants. These neighbors whose work puts food on our tables are often compelled to live without decent housing, schooling, health care and equal protection of the law.[15]

In addition to the needs of groups within our own boundaries, the whole human family calls to us for help.

Our allegiance must extend beyond the family and the nation to the entire human family. . . .

Human interdependence is constantly increasing in today's world, so that many issues which pertain to human dignity call for the collaboration of a true community of nations.[16]

To help the entire human family becomes a duty for us because of our unique position in the world:

Our nation's power, wealth, and position of leadership in the world impose special obligations upon us. Americans have always responded generously to foreign crises involving immediate human suffering: to floods and droughts, earthquakes and famines and the ravages of war. This is to our credit. But the obligations of which we now speak ex-

tend further. We must work creatively for a ju
tional order based on recognition of interdepend

One way to help people understand the import
international order is to propose the following exercise: "Here are
five countries differing in geography, history, military power, natural resources, and economy. You are to determine a series of
equitable economic and political relationships among them. Only
when you are finished, will we inform you to which country you
belong!" If citizens of a powerful country were faced with the
possibility of being *recipients* of their country's foreign policy
(political and economic), they would quickly find themselves having a great interest in whether that policy was just or not.

In the spirit of fairness the document continues:

> Such discussion of rules for relationships and the distribu-
> tion of power on the international level may be new to us as
> Americans but the themes are familiar to our experience.
> The American tradition emphasizes that rules of fairness
> are central to a just political system. The developing coun-
> tries argue that it is precisely rules of fairness in economic
> relations which do not now exist. Similarly, their quest for a
> new and more equitable form of bargaining power in rela-
> tion to us echoes the drive for bargaining power by Ameri-
> can workers over the last century.[18]

Nuclear weapons are not only a horrendous threat as a result of
their massive destructive capability but they are also bleeding dry
resources that could be used for human development. The cost of
one of the latest nuclear submarines could provide the funds to
build 450,000 modest homes. There are enough nuclear weapons
in the world to kill every person twelve times. There are approximately 30,000 nuclear weapons in the hands of the United States
with 615,000 times the destructive power of Hiroshima. In the
light of this the document continues:

> We urge the continued development and implementation of
> policies which seek to bring these weapons more securely
> under control, progressively reduce their presence in the
> world, and ultimately remove them entirely.[19]

Finally, the document calls our attention to the role of the United States in furthering human rights:

> This nation's traditional commitment to human rights may be its most significant contribution to world politics. Today, when rights are violated on the left and the right of the international political spectrum, the pervasive presence of our nation's political power and influence in the world provides a further opportunity and obligation to promote human rights. . . .
>
> There is a direct, decisive bond between the values we espouse in our nation and the world we seek to build internationally. When human rights are violated anywhere without protest, they are threatened everywhere. Our own rights are less secure if we condone or contribute even by passive silence to the repression of human rights in other countries.[20]

•

Another document deserving of consideration is *Political Responsibility: Choices for the 1980's* (Statement of the Administrative Board of the United States Catholic Conference, October 26, 1979). It contains a summary of various statements issued in recent years:

> Many of our citizens have simply thrown up their hands and turned away from politics and government *per se*. . . .
>
> The sensible response is to return to citizenship with the will and dedication to breathe new life into it. . . .[21]
>
> The application of Gospel values to real situations is an essential work of the Christian community. Christians believe the Gospel is the measure of human realities.[22]

Some of the issues to which the document then addresses itself are as follows:

> It is important to call attention to the fact that millions of Americans are still poor, jobless, hungry and inadequately housed and that vast disparities of income and wealth remain within our nation. These conditions are intolerable

and must be persistently challenged so that the economy will reflect a fundamental respect for the human dignity and basic needs of all. . . .[23]

We advocate sufficient public and private funding to make an adequate education available for all citizens and residents of the United States of America and to provide assistance for education in our nation's program of foreign aid. . . .[24]

Internationally, U.S. food aid should effectively combat global hunger and malnutrition, be aimed primarily at the poorest countries and neediest people without regard to political considerations. . . .[25]

It is not sufficient merely to aid these countries. Keeping in mind what has been stated earlier in these social documents, we must strive to bring about economic empowerment:

Economic assistance should emphasize helping other nations move toward food self-sufficiency.[26]

The document then goes on to list additional goals:

Adequate health care is an essential element in maintaining a decent standard of living. Yet the high costs of health care and uneven access to basic health resources make it impossible for many in our society to meet their basic health needs. . . .

Human dignity requires the defense and promotion of human rights in global and domestic affairs. With respect to international human rights, there is a pressing need for the U.S. to pursue a double task: (1) to strengthen and expand international mechanisms by which human rights can be protected and promoted; and (2) to take seriously the human rights dimensions of U.S. foreign policy. . . .

In Central America challenges to long-standing patterns of injustice and domination of large sectors of the population have been met by brutal repression. Fundamental social, economic and political changes advocated by the Church at the Puebla Conference call us in the U.S. to examine how our policies of military assistance and economic investment are related to existing patterns of injustice. U.S. policy should be directed toward fostering peaceful but fundamental change designed to benefit the poor of Central America.

This is not an exclusive listing of the issues that concern us. As Pope John Paul II has said, "The Church cannot remain insensible to whatever serves true human welfare any more than she can remain indifferent to whatever threatens it. . . ."[27]

•

The entire church can benefit from the riches of the Puebla Conference (Third General Conference of the Latin American Episcopate, Puebla, Mexico, January 27–February 13, 1979). Pope John Paul II in his opening address at Puebla stated:

> The whole Church owes you a debt of gratitude for what you are doing, for the example you are giving. Perhaps other local Churches will take up that example.[28]

Archbishop John Quinn of San Francisco in addressing the National Conference of U.S. Catholic Bishops (May 1979) called Puebla, "An event of major significance for us. But now comes the question, pointed and obvious: What effect will Puebla have on us?" The then president of the U.S. Bishops' Conference went on to say, "Puebla's analysis of Latin American reality is an invitation to us to assess with the key of revelation and the teaching of the Church the reality of the Church in our own situation."[29]

Puebla reminds us once again of the cry of many for their basic heart wishes:

> A little more than ten years ago, the Medellín Conference noted: "A muted cry wells up from millions of human beings, pleading with their pastors for a liberation that is nowhere to be found in their case" (88).
>
> The cry might well have been muted back then. Today it is loud and clear, increasing in volume and intensity, and at times full of menace (89).[30]

Listening to this cry, the church must ask itself certain questions:

> How has the Church viewed this reality? . . . Has the
> Church been successful in finding some way to focus on it
> and clarify it in the light of the Gospel (74)?[31]

In attempting to answer these self-imposed questions, the church reminds itself that the justice and peace apostolate is a necessary outgrowth of our participation in the inner love life of the Trinity:

> Christ reveals to us that the divine life is trinitarian communion. Father, Son, and Spirit live the supreme mystery of oneness in perfect, loving intercommunion. It is the source of all love and all other communion that gives dignity and grandeur to human existence (212).
>
> The communion that is to be fashioned between human beings is one that embraces their whole being, right down to the roots of their love. It must also manifest itself in every aspect of life, including economic, social, and political life (215).
>
> Evangelization prompts us to share in the groanings of the Spirit, who wishes to liberate all creation (219).

We see that the full meaning of evangelization must encompass human development and liberation:

> Evangelization introduces Jesus as the Lord who reveals the Father to us and shares his Spirit with us (352).
>
> The salvation offered to us by Christ gives meaning to all human aspirations and achievement . . . (253).
>
> This salvation, the Center of the Good News, is liberation from everything that oppresses the human being (354).

In traditional theology we are concerned with realized eschatology and final eschatology. In terms of realized eschatology we rejoice in what Christ accomplished during the time of his original earthly mission. In terms of final eschatology we await what Christ will accomplish at the end of time. All of this is true and wonderful, but it is not the whole truth nor the full wonder. If we have only this traditional view of realized and final eschatology, we are left stranded in the here and now with a basically passive attitude and static mind-set. What we need is a *realizing* eschatology in which we see ourselves as co-evolvers with Christ in his ongoing work. The more we cooperate in justice and peace activities, the more we further Christ's evolutionary task and bring about a foretaste of the ultimate evolution in the present.

In carrying out this evolutionary task, the church seeks to evangelize cultures:

> Evangelization seeks to get to the very core of a culture, the realm of its basic values, and to bring about a conversion that will serve as the basis and guarantee of a tranformation in structures and the social milieu (388).

> Cultures are continually subjected to new developments and to mutual encounter and interpenetration. In the course of their history they go through periods in which they are challenged by new values or disvalues, and by the need to effect new syntheses of their way of life. The Church feels particularly summoned to make its presence felt, to be there with the Gospel, when old ways of social life and value-organization are decaying or dying in order to make room for new syntheses (393).

The church is challenging the message of those who uphold an unjust state of affairs in any culture. In order to protect their power position in an unjust situation, they send out a message that defends present conditions. As Janeway states:

> The message runs something like this: if you join with others in bands that reject the established and orthodox social structure and the mythology that sustains it, you are venturing into a howling wilderness of sects and cults where no maps exist. . . . Better, far better, to restrain your feelings and modify your desires and ambitions, better to take as a guide some practical manual on how to make it, "the company way" and satisfy your aspirations by finding a comfortable niche in the here and now.

This is of course the sort of message which any Establishment is always beaming out to its audience.[32]

Those suffering from injustice must be challenged both to evaluate and rise above the status quo. The weak must be helped to see that one of the reasons they often unquestioningly adhere to a structure that oppresses them is that they have been indoctrinated from childhood to accept it. A maturing process must take place. Those in ministry must help the oppressed to have "the encounter with experiences or perspectives that leads to a critical reflection on how one's beliefs and values have formed . . . and how relative they are to one's particular group or background."[33]

The Puebla document calls for evangelizing action in challenging all forms of systemic violence:

> Recent years have seen a growing deterioration in the socio-political life of our countries (507).
>
> They are experiencing the heavy burden of economic and institutional crises, and clear symptoms of corruption and violence (508).
>
> This violence is generated and fostered by two factors: (1) what can be called institutionalized injustice in various social, political, and economic systems; and (2) ideologies that use violence as a means to win power (509).
>
> The latter in turn causes the proliferation of governments based on force, which often derive their inspiration from the ideology of National Security (510).[34]

The above-mentioned doctrine of national security (*seguridad nacional*) maintains that for the security of the state it is necessary to hold the vast majority of the people under the control of a small elite who exercise all power. Such reasoning, of course, leads to the greatest of abuses regarding human rights.

The consideration of women's rights was, unfortunately, very limited at Puebla, but the document states:

> We must consider *the equality and dignity of the woman*. Like man, the woman is the image of God: "God created man in his image; in the divine image he created him; male

and female he created them" (Gen. 1:27). Thus the task of ruling the world, continuing the work of creation, and being God's co-creators is woman's as much as man's (841).

The document calls attention to the fact that women in oppressed groups are also oppressed *within* their groups. As a result, the women of these groups "are doubly oppressed and marginalized" (1134n.).

Puebla expresses clearly a preferential option for the poor:

When we draw near to the poor in order to accompany them and serve them, we are doing what Christ taught us to do when he became our brother, poor like us . . . the best service to our fellows is evangelization, which disposes them to fulfill themselves as children of God, liberates them from injustices, and fosters their integral advancement (1147).

Commitment to the poor and oppressed and the rise of grassroots communities have helped the Church to discover the evangelizing potential of the poor. For the poor challenge the Church constantly, summoning it to conversion; and many of the poor incarnate in their lives the evangelical values of solidarity, service, simplicity, and openness to accepting the gift of God (1147).

Committed to the poor, we condemn as anti-evangelical the extreme poverty that affects an extremely large segment of the population on our continent (1159).

We will make every effort to understand and denounce the mechanisms that generate this poverty (1160).

The Puebla document concludes with a challenge to both its authors and to us:

We Christians, in our role as the People of God, are sent out to be a truly reliable seed of unity, hope, and salvation (1301).

We opt for a missionary Church that joyously proclaims to the people today that they are children of God in Christ, that commits itself to the liberation of the whole human being and all human beings; service to peace and justice is an essential ministry of the Church (1304).

These attitudes . . . call for a Church engaged in an on-going process of evangelization; an evangelized Church that heeds, explores, and incarnates the divine Word. . . . This same evangelizing Church must also help to construct a new society in complete fidelity to Christ and humanity in the Holy Spirit . . . *committing believers to world-transforming action* (1305) [Italics added].

In this appendix we have seen proof of a truly remarkable emergence in the church: its rising conscientization regarding justice and peace. Much, of course, has yet to be done. But the fact remains that a quantum leap has taken place, and neither the church nor the world will ever be the same again. Once conscientization has been experienced in people's hearts, it cannot be suppressed. It can only reach new heights and spread far and wide. Who could have imagined what would happen in the next two decades when John XXIII issued his first social encyclical? What potentialities exist for the next two decades! The challenge for action in development, liberation, justice, and peace summons us on.

Notes to Appendix A

1. The English translation of *Mater et Magistra* is by William Gibbons, S.J., and was published by the Paulist Press, Glen Rock, N.J., in 1961. The numerals in parentheses refer to the paragraph numbers introduced into the encyclical by Father Gibbons. This document (and many of the other documents quoted in Appendix A) are reprinted in Joseph Gremillion, ed., *The Gospel of Peace and Justice: Catholic Social Teaching Since Pope John XXIII* (Maryknoll, N.Y.: Orbis Books, 1976).

2. Elizabeth Janeway, *Powers of the Weak* (New York: Alfred A. Knopf, 1980), p. 6.

3. *Mater et Magistra.*

4. Janeway, *Powers of the Weak,* p. 132.

5. The English text of *Pacem in Terris* was published by the America Press, New York, 1963. Reprinted in Gremillion, *The Gospel of Peace and Justice.*

6. Janeway, *Powers of the Weak,* p. 84.

7. *Pacem in Terris.*

8. The English version used here (and for all the documents of Vatican II quoted in this volume) is taken from Walter M. Abbot, S.J., *The Documents of Vatican II* (New York: America Press, 1966). All these documents are reprinted in Gremillion, *The Gospel of Peace and Justice.*

9. The English version used here was published by the Vatican Polyglot Press in booklet form, 62 pages. A.A.S. LIX (April 15, 1967), no. 4, pp. 257–99. Reprinted in Gremillion, *The Gospel of Peace and Justice.*

10. Janeway, *Powers of the Weak,* p. 150.

11. This English version was published by the Vatican Polyglot Press in booket form, 70 pages. A.A.S. LXIII (June 30, 1971), no. 6, pp. 401–41. Reprinted in Gremillion, *The Gospel of Peace and Justice.*

12. *Evangelii Nuntiandi: On Evangelization in the Modern World* (Washington, D.C.: United States Catholic Conference Publications Office, 1976).

13. *Crux,* December 13, 1976, pp. 1–2.

14. *Crux,* December 20, 1976, p. 5.

15. Ibid., pp. 5–6.

16. Ibid., p. 6.

17. Ibid.

18. Ibid., p. 7.

19. Ibid.

20. Ibid.

21. *Political Responsibility: Choices for the 1980's* (Washington, D.C.: United States Catholic Conference Publications Office, 1979), p. 7.

22. Ibid., p. 10.

23. Ibid., p. 7.

24. Ibid., p. 10.

25. Ibid., p. 12.

26. Ibid.

27. Ibid., pp. 12–14.

28. In John Eagleson and Philip Scharper, eds. *Puebla and Beyond* (Maryknoll, N.Y.: Orbis Books, 1979), p. 58.

29. Ibid., p. 328.

30. Ibid., p. 134.

31. Ibid., p. 132.

32. Janeway, *Powers of the Weak,* p. 184.

33. James Fowler, "Faith and the Structuring of Meaning" in *Toward Religious Maturity* (Morristown, N.J.: Silver Burdett Company, 1980), p. 71.

34. *Puebla and Beyond,* pp. 194–95.

Appendix B

ADDITIONAL READINGS AND RESOURCES

Books

Corson-Finnerty, Adam Daniel. *World Citizen: Action for Global Justice* (Maryknoll, N.Y.: Orbis Books, 1982). For those who want to become involved with action groups, this book provides helpful background essays and an exceptionally comprehensive sixty-page annotated listing of action groups and resources.

DiGiacomo, S.J., James, and Walsh, M.M., John. *The Encounter Series: The Longest Step, Meet the Lord,* and *Going Together* with three accompanying resource manuals. Minneapolis: Winston Press, 1978. A detailed unfolding of an evangelization process now in use in schools and parishes of the United States and several other countries.

Fowler, Jim, and Keen, Sam. *Life Maps: Conversations on the Journey of Faith.* Minneapolis: Winston Press, 1978. Jim Fowler presents his theory of faith maturity. Sam Keen responds by offering a more holistic approach. Afterwards both authors engage in a dialogue.

Fowler, James W. *Stages of Faith.* San Francisco: Harper & Row, 1981. A more elaborate treatment of the concept of faith and its development.

Fowler, James W., and Lovin, Robin W. *Trajectories in Faith.* Nashville: Abingdon Press, 1980. The faith development theory is here applied to the life stories of Dietrich Bonhoeffer, Anne Hutchinson, Blaise Pascal, Ludwig Wittgenstein, and Malcolm X.

Articles

DiGiacomo, S.J., James. "Evangelizing the Young." *America,* October 13, 1979: 187–89. Why evangelization is necessary for the young and not-so-young.
———. "Why Johnny Can't Pray." *America,* December 10, 1977: 414–18. An explanation of the pivotal states—Stages Three, Four, and Five—of Fowler's theory of faith maturity.
Walsh, M.M., John. "Evangelization and Parish Renewal." *Ministries* (1980): 4–5. A correlation between the evangelization process and the New Rite of Initiation of Adults. According to the new rite, the parish community should undergo the ritual along with prospective converts. As a result, the evangelization experience will become the core of a parish renewal.

Films

All these films are suggested for use with *The Encounter Series:*

Baptism. Produced by Teleketics, 1229 South Santee Street, Los Angeles, CA 90015. A wandering boy symbolizes the process of coming to Baptism. Recommended for use with Chapter 5 of *Going Together.*
Jesus, B.C. Produced by Insight, Paulist Productions, 17575 Pacific Coast Highway, Pacific Palisades, CA 90272. The Trinity plans the Incarnation. Although the dialogue is light in tone, a sophisticated theology underlies the film, which is recommended for use at the beginning of *Meet the Lord.*
The Rebirth of Packy Rowe. Produced by Insight, Paulist Productions, 17575 Pacific Coast Highway, Pacific Palisades, CA 90272. This film, which stars Jack Klugman and Bob Newhart, can be used with Chapter 4 of *Going Together.* Its subject is an apparent failure who reexamines his life.

The Red Kite. Produced by Wombat, P.O. Box 70, Glendale Road, Ossining, NY 10562. An account of the search for God and the meaning of life. Can be used at the beginning of *The Longest Step.*

A Slight Change in Plans. Insight, Paulist Productions, 17575 Pacific Coast Highway, Pacific Palisades, CA 90272. What is priesthood about? Can be used in connection with Chapter 13 of *Going Together.*

Cassettes

Coming to Faith: The Dynamics of Evangelization. Produced by National Catholic Reporter Cassettes, Box 281, Kansas City, Missouri 64141. These eight cassettes contain lectures by Jim DiGiacomo, S.J., and John Walsh, M.M., for the Fordham University Graduate School of Religion and Religious Education. (A set of *The Encounter Series* is included in the kit.)